Enjoy the Social History
in the Maps,
Paddy Wahl

DEDICATION

This book is dedicated to the preservation of local historical material relevant to Kiltimagh, Co Mayo, Ireland, dating from 1792 to 2021.

JERRY WALSH

FAMILY-MAN, MERCHANT, HISTORIAN, AUTHOR, FRIEND

Jerry Walsh was born on the 23rd of October 1918, he was the third son of Michael Patrick (MP) Walsh and Mary Ellen O'Hora. Jerry had two brothers, John Joe and Paddy. This book is a compilation of Jerry's poetry, presenting his perspective of the issues and activities of the town of Kiltimagh, Co Mayo, and its people in the turbulent times before Ireland was declared free.

Where possible and at the start of each poem a brief introduction has been added in order to explain what was happening at that time and to provide a guide to some of the context, background information and motivation for each poem.

From an early age, Jerry and his Walsh Family at the corner house, owned and ran a shop. This included a travelling shop visiting houses in and around Kiltimagh. and in the East Mayo area down the boreens and byways where migration for seasonal work sent the men to work in places like Yorkshire and the cities of England. The Irish country women would barter eggs for groceries like Tea and essentials. This was a wonderful service for the country breadwinning women when mobility was an issue. It boosted the Family income depending on the number of eggs they could sell, these eggs were then boxed and exported via Ballina and Sligo to England where the Walsh's had a shop in Bradford.

During this time, Jerry got to know the grandparents, most of the families and the hordes of children in each village. This knowledge was to prove invaluable in later years when Jerry opened the Raftery Room providing music and entertainment in 1959. Not only did he know these people, his customers he had also bought eggs from their mothers and grandmothers.

Jerry Walsh was trustworthy and dependable, his personality was "Larger than Life" and his love of people was genuine. Jerry's hobbies were Tennis, Fishing, Reading Poetry, Films Boxing and particularly Gene Tunney the Long Count and Gerry Cooney the Great White Hope. After Patrick and Marcella Reilly opened their tennis court and ice cream shop in Aiden Street, Jerry became an enthusiastic and regular member of this Club. Some years later, this Tennis Club was continued at the top of the town in Gortgarve by Paddy Forde. We all miss Jerry Walsh, and this is our tribute to him.

TABLE OF CONTENTS

TABLE OF FIGURES

ACKNOWLEDGMENTS

First, I would like to thank my family: Melanie for advising me to record those events, otherwise future generations may not be aware of family history. Sandra for her recommendations on structure and editing, and Eamonn, Trudi and Lena for their support and encouragement. I am profoundly grateful to my siblings: Sean, Celia, Jer, Pierce (RIP), Barry, Nathy, Damien for their continued interest and guidance and to my brother Tony for his skills on publication.

I would also like to thank Mary and Pat Salmon from Knock, for supplying their kitchen table for tea, food and healthy discussion on innumerable occasions, and for confirmation and verification issues.

I would like to thank Jim Lunden for editing, and Aiden Burke for helpful advice. For the provision of photos: I would like to thank Basil Burke, Alan Driver, Susan Carroll, Anne Forde.

Tom Jordan and Michael Commins, The Mayo News. The Western People and James Laffey.

I would like to extend my gratitude to Jackie Kelly, MSLETB, ICT lecturer at Coláiste Raftéirí, Kiltimagh, our most capable teacher for her exceptional patience and outstanding efforts and who pioneered the idea that learners should consider writing a book after completing their ICT Certificates.

Finally, I would like to thank all my friends from the ICT classes for their continuous support.

PRESIDENT JOHN F. KENNEDY

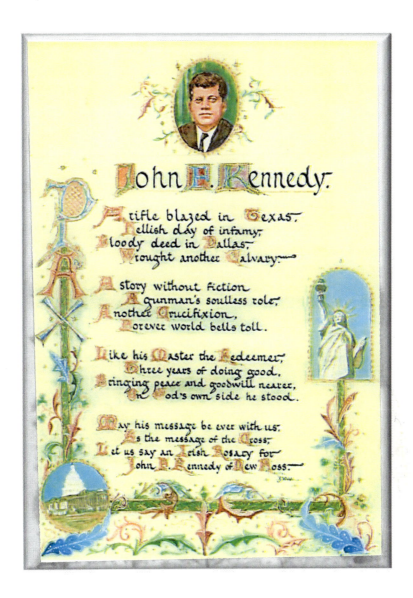

Figure 1 Designed, scrolled, and painted by
Katie Casby from Knock. Poem by Jerry Walsh

THE BOYS FROM THE COUNTY MAYO

From Midfield to Woodfield from Greyfield to Cragga,
Cloonkedagh, Cloondoolagh and old Cultibo,
Treenlaur and Treenkeel, Treenagleragh, Teenfaughnane,
Reared the best hearted men from the County Mayo.

For football or handball, for boxing or working,
The men of Kil-tim-agh, smashed records you know,
They defeated the best men, they were never Yes-Yes men,
Historians still praise them when they write of Mayo.

Our famous Gene Tunney, who beat old Jack Dempsey,
Owes a debt to Kil-tim-agh, his parents you know,
The Lydon's Gortgarve, and the Tunney's Cultrasna,
They too were exiled from the County Mayo.

Seán Lavan the Champion, the pride of all Ireland,
Whose toe to hand movement, changed football you know,
His wind it surprised them, his speed it defied them,
With that Forde drop inside him when he played for Mayo.

From Historic Killaiden, the home of old Raftery,
Who taught us our music, before the Fleadh-Ceoil,
His Anois teach Earraigh beidh an lá dul cun sineadh,
The scholars are still singing his Condae Mhuigeo.

The days of our youth we will never forget them,
As we danced the old half sets and lancers also.
With the bagpipes and hornpipes,
we had had none of these drainpipes,
We had plenty of claypipes in the County Mayo.

2

So, away to the Congo with those Rumbos and Tangos,
The rock and roll music we'll banish also,
Ceoltas Tire are ready to catch the first Teddy.
Who brings the Twist in to the County Mayo!

Sean Lavan and "the toe to hand movement"

Jerry Walsh composed this poem about the boys from Kiltimagh in the East Mayo section of the County of Mayo. The mayo news wrote on 7 May 2013 that Tom Dunleavy Writer and Poet from Kiltimagh, County Mayo, Ireland was the man who composed "The Boys from the County Mayo" in New York in the early 1930s, he was an immigrant who had taken those great words to his heart 'Don't show the white feather wherever you go'. He had more than proved himself to be one of the 'true-hearted men from the County Mayo'.

Kiltimagh is in the Civil and R C Parish of Killedan aka Killaiden, the villages mentioned below Greyfield, Cloondoolagh, Cultrasna, Treenagleragh, Gortgarve, Cordarragh are in Killedan parish. Midfield is in the adjoining parish of Kilconduff. Woodfield is in Kilkelly parish formerly Aghamore parish.

Figure 2 Dr Seán Lavan Kiltimagh and Mayo GAA

This unique skill and an integral part of Gaelic football, the 'solo run' is a thrilling spectacle when played at speed and executed with tantalising side step and body swerve. This particular art was initiated by Séan Lavan a Mayo doctor from Kiltimagh, who was the Garda Surgeon for many years, described as the "toe-to-hand" by the late Micheál O'Hehir.

He also represented the new Republic of Ireland in its very first venture into the Olympic Games in 1923, which were held in Paris that year.

The holder of 180 medals altogether, for

athletic and field events, Seán Lavan also captained the Irish Olympic Team in 1928. Dr. Seán Lavan was the Medical Officer to the Irish Team at the Melbourne Olympic Games of 1956, where Ronnie Delaney took gold. But Seán was especially renowned for his ball control and juggling skills. He told of an occasion during that game when he had the ball in his possession and had used up his permitted quota of ball bounces. At that time, the rules permitted two or three successive ball bounces, after which the ball had to be released or kicked to a fellow player.

The 'Baller Lavan' was well positioned and wanted to hold possession for a little while longer, so he took the decision to kick the ball gently into the air and catch it himself. He tried this out and the referee did not blow the whistle for a foul or penalise him. The 'Baller' repeated the action and then passed to an incoming forward, who subsequently kicked the ball over the bar for the winning point.

Figure 3 Opening of Kiltimagh Museum June 1989 by
Tom Flatley from Treenkeel and Boston

L to R: Tom Flatley, Eneas Kelly, Michael O'Malley, John Joe McNicholas,
Jerry Walsh, Tommy Carney, Michael D. Freeley, Paddy Reilly,
John Joe McNamara, Noel Mulhern, Heny King.

CAPTAIN PA DUNLEAVEY OF THE EAST MAYO BRIGADE

In a graveyard in Bohola our gallant comrade lies,
Beside the place that gave him birth, beneath his Irish skies,
He fought to free his native land when his country was betrayed,
He is Captain Pa Dunleavy of the East Mayo Brigade.

He raised that flag of freedom on a banner proud and high,
He helped to beat the Black and Tans,
He taught them how to die,
He led Bohola Company, and many attacks were made,
By Captain Pa Dunleavy of the East Mayo Brigade.

'Twas on a Sunday morning they attacked Ballyvary town,
And took the guns and barracks from the forces of the crown,
When they captured Charlestown, the shoneens were afraid,
Of Captain Pa Dunleavy of the East Mayo Brigade.

On the slopes of old Slieve Horn when his men laid down to rest,
Dunleavey held the enemy, one man against the rest,
When his rifle went on fire with flame, a prisoner then was made,
Of Captain Pa Dunleavy of the East Mayo Brigade.

In Sligo jail they held him, Kilmainham and Athlone,
In Longford, Galway and Mountjoy no braver man was known,
In the Tin Town on the Curragh, mighty men have prayed,
With Captain Pa Dunleavy of the East Mayo Brigade.

We salute you gallant sentry, as the bravest and best,
On that hillside in Bohola that forever shall be blest,
God guard and keep our comrade, whose name shall never fade,
The name of Pa Dunleavy of the East Mayo Brigade.

Obituary of Pa Dunleavy

We regret to announce the death of Captain Patrick Dunleavy, o/c Bohola Company, 3rd Batt East Mayo Brigade Old I.R.A. who died at Mater Hospital, Dublin, on 20th May 1961. The deceased was attached to the Department of Agriculture and lived in Dublin for several years. He was a pioneer of the volunteer movement and took part in all major engagements in the Brigade area and was a gallant and sterling soldier. He was a much-wanted man in the fight for independence in the Black and Tan period and was in the attack and capture of Ballyvary R.I.C. Barracks in 1920, and in the attack on Ballaghaderreen R.I.C. Barracks in 1921.

The deceased was attached to the 3rd Western Active Service Unit stationed at Boyle and fought with his unit on the Republican side during the civil war and took part in the attack and capture of Swinford Garrison. Later he fought at Ballinamore until his ammunition became exhausted and was taken prisoner and interned in Ballina, Galway, Kilmainham and Curragh jails. During his imprisonment he endured a prolonged hunger strike which had an adverse effect on his health, and which aggravated by a bullet wound, impaired his constitution and shortened his life. The bullet removed from his spine many years later, is retained by his wife, Mrs. Delia Dunleavy. He is survived by his wife, and his four sisters, Mrs. Annie Boyle, Mrs. Margaret Gordon, and Mrs. Mary Hogquist, all in U.S.A., and Miss Julia Dunleavy, of County Mayo.

The attendance at Dublin obsequies and removal of the remains to Bohola Parish Church included Mr. M. O'Cleraigh, County Registrar, Dublin, former Chief of Staff, I.R.A.; Mr. Thomas Loftus, Superintendent Leinster House; Mr. Seán Walsh, Mr. Seamus Kilcullen, Mr. Henry McNicholas, Mr. Patrick Hyland, Mr. Seán Gibbons, Mr. Peadar Glynn, Mr. Frank Colgan, all former high-ranking I.R.A. officers in Mayo.

At Swinford the Old I.R.A. formed a guard of honour and marched beside the hearse through the town. Solemn Requiem Mass was celebrated for the repose of his soul by Very Rev. Canon Durcan, P.P., Bohola, Rev. Fr Henry, C.C. (deacon), and Rev. Fr O'Hara (sub-deacon). The funeral took place to the family burial ground, Bohola Cemetery, escorted by a guard of honour and firing party under the command of Officers Dunleavy, Walsh and Colgan, led by Pipers T. Maloney and A. Lyons, playing the funeral march. Fr Henry, C.C., officiated at the graveside and recited a decade of the Rosary in Irish. Three volleys were fired over the grave and the Last Post sounded by Mr. C. Cunningham, Swinford. The firing party, under the command of Commandant Seán Walsh, comprised of: Henry McNichols, Patrick Hyland, Martin Gordon, William Foley, Thomas Price, Sean Robinson.

Figure 4 Patrick Dunleavy
1889-1961 Delia Roache

JOHN FORDE
FROM OLD CLOONDOOLAGH WAY

Air: McNamara's Band

His name is Sergeant John, the best Sergeant of his day,
When he paid the boys in Kevin Street, no guard was turned away,
He then set sail for the country, his own beloved West,
From Galway, Sligo to Listowel, he loved Cloondoolagh best.

He has a good man down there, to manage his famous farm,
That man's name is 'Sniper' nothing will ever harm,
The bullocks or the heifers, its full of springers too,
To men like that, take off your hat, those brave Cloondoolagh two.

When we had the fairs in Kiltimagh, John Forde stood on the street,
He didn't need an auctioneer to make the deal complete,
He told the buyers stand four square, you need no scales to weigh,
Those strippers they were born and bulled the old Cloondoolagh way.

And then he told them other things, how good men should be reared,
How the men from Cloondoolagh, around the world have fared,
For working or for drinking, or keeping the ball in play,
They were bred the best; they beat the rest down old Cloondoolagh way.

When the times changed around, the marts came on the scene,
John Forde stood in in Kiltimagh, the last seller to be seen,
He stood his ground: he bought his round,
and blasted things called marts,
We heard him say; "you'll rue the day, they'll break the farmers hearts".

This evening we are gathered here in dear old Dublin town,
To pay respect and homage to a man of great renown,
That man's name is John Forde, may his memory ever stay,
In the hearts of all who love him and his own Cloondoolagh way.

8

Figure 5 John Thomas Forde 1912-1989
Cloondoolagh, Dublin, Kiltimagh

Born in the village of Cloondoolagh, Kiltimagh John Thomas Forde 1912-1989 (the Son of Ned Forde 1880-1965 and Anne Sweeney 1873-1953) John's 2nd marriage was to Marcella Gormally 1934-2012 who was the Matron of Mayo General Hospital, Castlebar. John inherited the family farm, and his heart was in Farming, his good neighbour was Thomas Brennan aka 'Sniper' and he also his friend, the two men worked well together John was the brother of Eamon Forde.

A Bullock is a castrated male animal, a heifer is a young female animal before she has had a calf, a springer is a cow or heifer close to calfing, a stripper is a cow well past her prime.

IRISH SPINNERS LTD

You've heard of Irish Spinners, sure they're spinners of renown,
They spin the finest yarns in there, the best that can be found,
They even beat old Dingo, and challenge him they will,
At spinning yarns, the finest yarns, on Farrell Cunnane's Hill.

It started up in Dublin, not many months ago,
Dáil Eireann passed that Bill first time for factories in Mayo,
Ballyhaunis, Swinford, Ballinrobe, they certainly did their best,
But Kil-tim-agh fought, Kil-tim-agh brought that factory to the West.

Roughneen went up to Dublin, it's not so long ago,
With Gilmartin, Gaynor and McNally to the Department they did go,
They told Lemass that Coillte-mac was always staunch and true,
They nearly died when Lemass cried "Me Coillte-mac man too".

When the hill came down, the scaffolds went up,
Mick Meenaghan took command,
He built that factory there, the finest in the land,
And when he had it finished, he said; "This didn't pay",
He went for a cure and a ten-week tour of the grand old USA.

And then we met the quiet man, O'Reilly Hyland was his name,
When he bought our shares, we said our prayers,
that the mill would be the same,
"Not the same" he said, "but bigger, we'll have to increase output,
We'll fight the Common Market with a group called Readicut".

We've Mick Lavin there from Churchpark, and men from Aiden Street,
And fifty more from around our town have emigration beat,
They're working there from Foxford, and Bohola of renown,
They're a credit to old Ireland and won't let Herman down.

With a "Driver" and an "Iredale", Sure, the job it must be right,
The orders are so big, sure they're working day and night,
We are proud of Irish Spinners and so we sing our song,
To show the rest of Ireland, that OLD COILLTE MARCHES ON.

**Figure 6 Fred Driver MD Irish Spinners and Cordarragh
Kiltimagh**

**Figure 8 Herman Armitage
Irish Spinners Kiltimagh**

**Figure 7 Clara & Stephen Iredale
Irish Spinners Station Road
Kiltimagh**

SAVOY CINEMA

Background

The New Savoy Cinema was built on the site of the former Queens Commercial Hotel, previously owned by James Dolphin and his family at the corner of Main Street and Thomas Street, Kiltimagh. When opened in 1944, it had 600 seats including a balcony and the sound system was an Ernemann, later called RCA, sound. It closed in the 1970's and was converted into Kiltimagh Community Centre which opened in October 1977.

The Idea of a Cinema came from a quartet of local people three of these men had local and long-established businesses in the area: these were James B (Jimmy) Lavin, Charles Gilmartin and JP Roughneen the fourth man was local Doctor Anthony Kirby. The Meenaghan Brothers were the main contractors, Walter Dwyer a plumber, Jimmy Kelly an electrician and Jimmy Duddy a carpenter worked on the site.

Johnny Carroll from Thomas Street cycled daily to Ballinrobe where he learned the trade of projectionist. His assistants were Johnny Kelly and TJ Mullaney from Aiden St.

Historian Aiden Burke reveals that four old pence bought you a place on the congested and uncomfortable hard benches next to the screen, nine pence secured an individual softer seat further away from the screen, and if you had a shilling and three old pence in your hand, then you were the envy of many when you climbed the stairs to the balcony with its tip-up seats and ashtrays.

The Savoy was normally full and not a seat to spare. Mick Higgins patrolled the aisles, while the latest hits were playing on an old 78 record player. A buzz of excitement would sweep through the building, the lights would go down and at the same time a beam of light from the projection room would light up the screen. An immediate hush would follow as the marvel of the big screen played out before the eyes of the excited patrons. Trailers of films to come would whet their appetites. Next the advertisements followed, and lastly the long-awaited film exploded on the screen- it is:
The Lost Feathers!

There was a great sense of disappointment and withdrawal when the film ended, and the bright lights went up, the world of reality is back, and the two hours of escapism are over.

JP Roughneen's wife Joan was a member of the McNally family from Westport, the well-known film distributers, so the Kiltimagh Savoy always got the new films next after Dublin. Walt Disney visited them in the Roughneen private residence in Thornton House in Gortgarve, with the party in full swing it attracted the attention of the local guard O'Connor who was informed the visitors were arriving directly from Hollywood in California. Guard O'Connor quipped back that he was O'Connor and that his direct ancestors were the High Kings of Ireland. Two red bulbs flashed on and off on either side of the big screen to alert local fire brigade members to report to the local fire station if there was a fire in the locality.

Figure 9 Kiltimagh Community Centre formerly Savoy Cinema

SAVOY CINEMA

For years we heard of talkies, and of cinemas afar,
If we wanted to see a picture, sure, we had to hire a car,
The war came on, the juice went scarce, and many a night was spent,
On walking the streets of Kiltimagh, on entertainment bent.

When the Queens came down, the scaffolds went up,
Jack Meenaghan took command,
He built the cinema there on the spot, the finest in the land,
JP, Tony, Jimmy and Charlie, they were the real McCoy.
They surely turned the corner, boys! into the new Savoy.

Of troubles and worries, the directors had their share,
The ESB just blacked them out, they said they didn't care,
But Lavan worked a Yankee Dodge, in true American style,
With Mullaney at the engine, she's good for many a mile.

When it comes to booking pictures, our directors don't delay,
Already we've got the 'Sullivans' and also 'Going my way',
They're trying hard for 'Gone with the Wind',
and 'the Song of Bernadette'.
And thousands more with stars galore, are coming our way yet.

Now to finish with my chorus, I wish you lots of joy,
I hope that you'll be happy here, in our lovely new Savoy,
We're proud of our directors, and so we sing this song,
To show the rest of Ireland, that Old Coillte marches on.

**Figure 10 Queen's Commercial Hotel later Savoy
Cinema the Kiltimagh Community Centre Photo
courtesy of Basil Burke**

MAYO FIRE BRIGADE

Figure 11 Moonlight in Mayo

You've heard of all the meetings, and discussions long ago,
About the aid of a fire brigade for the County of Mayo,
Then at last it took some councillors with courage staunch and true,
To meditate, shove up the rate, by another bob or two.

They advertised all over, at home and far away,
In search of a good firefighting man, who would do as they would say,
Sure, they found him up in Galway, after searching far and near,
He soon turned on the pressure for the County Engineer.

He was born in the Town of Tuam, where they make our sugar sweet,
And in his father's ovens, he first saw fire and heat,
And then he joined the army, a captain to become,
Sure, he made them walk, with Gaelic talk, in that well-known army tongue.

His name is Captain Garvey, he is a fire chief of renown,
He organised a firing squad, in every Mayo town,
With Rovers and equipment, and with lectures on first aid,
Sure, the best turned out in Ireland, is the Mayo Fire Brigade.

Tom Devereaux there in Castlebar, his name is French you see,
He must have come with Humbert's men, to set old Ireland free,
And Ballina are lucky, it would fill your heart with joy,
You'll always see, brave McElwee, in action on the Moy.

With John Joe Walsh in Kiltimagh-no day-old chick is he,
They say, he calls 'Chuck chuck, chuck, chuck, not 123 you see,
Ballyhaunis, Swinford, Ballinrobe and old Claremorris Town,
Have Grogan, Keane and Cunningham, and Gallagher of renown.

With Corcoran there in Westport, to man the Atlantic line,
Jo Byrne in Knock is guardian of, our Blessed Mary's Shrine,
When you hear the sirens wailing, like the banshee long ago,
Sure, its Garvey's men across the glen, when its moonlight in Mayo.

Now to finish with my chorus – I want you all "Make Down",
And have a right old Irish night in old Kiltimagh Town,
We're proud of Mayo Fire Brigade, -and so I'll sing this song,
To show the rest of Ireland, that mighty Mayo marches on.

Figure 12 Kiltimagh Fire Brigade

Back Row L to R: John Joe Walsh, Paddy Murtagh, Denny Charlton, Jimmy Kelly.
Front Row L to R: Billy Conroy, PJ Murtagh, Johnny Kelly and Michael Joe Kilduff.

COURSE NO. 10

Oh! Mary this brewery is a wonderful sight,
They are coming and going, by day and by night,
I can't just see how I will settle again,
When I finish this course, they call Number 10.

I am up in the morning at first break of day,
Every sunrise is another fair day,
I long to be home, to sleep till half ten,
But you can't do that here, on course Number 10.

Al Byrne met us all, up at the grand Cherry Tree,
You remember 'twas him, put the Tea on TV,
When Justin is around, you'll make no mistake,
Do you know what he calls it- a natural break.

They're teaching us all 'bout beer, music and snacks,
Management, insurance, dispensing and tax,
Wines and the cellar, where the profits are going,
We'd all know where we stood if we'd Jim Healy back home.

With Cocktails and Mussels, we talk of finance,
Soft drinks, and work study, and a licence to dance,
Presenting our pint, and controlling our stocks,
On security and hygiene, we must pull up our socks.

Now Mary 'a-grá', it's not a husband you've got,
But a brand-new Pub Manager, who knowns the whole lot,
If wild yeast in my dispenser, breaks out now and then,
You can blame Justin Collins and his course Number Ten.

With the compliments of Jerry Walsh, Raftery Room. Sung by 20 members
of the Course No. 10 at the presentation of Certificates in Guinness
Brewery in a hastily convened first 'Guinness Choir'.

Jerry Walsh at some time in 1960.

GARDEN CITY OF MELBOURNE

Farewell to old Ireland,
As blue skies I am flying across,
To the great garden city of Melbourne,
In the land of the Southern Cross.

Christmas hills forever are calling,
Beaming down on grand Yarra Glen,
To a rally in the valley recalling,
Great wines of the world once again.

To walk on the banks of the Yarra,
Where nature's wild beauty belongs,
Ever guarded by Wattle and Jarrah.
In the shadow of great Dandelongs.

As sun sets on lovely Olinda,
Yarra Ranges their secrets unveil,
Great memories of Dame Nellie Melba,
On the waters of Lake Lilydale.

We salute brave deeds of explorers,
World bells forever will ring,
And pay homage to great men before us,
To Burke – to Wills and to King.

GROW ON, LOVELY GARDENS OF MELBOURNE
ANZAC SPIRIT FOREVER WILL STAY
AT THE BIRTH OF THE NEW MILLENIUM
AS IT DAWNS ON PORT PHILLIP BAY

Figure 13 Melbourne Australia

18

AN OLD IRISH WEDDING TOAST

To the Bride and Groom,
Here's wishing you the best of luck,
Good luck to thee and thine,
Not only what is earthly,
But all that is divine.

May earth and heaven mingle,
May earth and heaven be one,
To guide you on life's journey,
Till sets your earthly sun.

May the hand that you have given,
And the hand that is given to you,
May both be joined together,
May both be good and true.

In sunshine or in shadow,
In sighing or in song,
May heavens bless your union,
Throughout your whole lives long.

Written by MP Walsh circa 1910
Father of Jerry Walsh

Beasty's Stout is good no doubt,
In either wood or bottle,
Her Bass's Ale would never fail,
To quench
A thirsty throttle.

As you slide down the bannisters of life,
May all the splinters,
be in the right direction.

Figure 14 Marriage 1914 MP Walsh and Mary Ellen O'Hora

Treenagleragh, Kiltimagh known locally as Slieve Horn, Slieve Carn (Sliabh Chairn in Irish, Mountain of the Cairn) it rises to 262 metres above sea level, at the top there was an ancient cremation area, the evidence of several burial site's was found there. Treenagleragh is one the villages near the top and it is also a Townland. It is adjacent to the Townland of Toochannagh where Mary Ellen Walsh nee O'Hora was born. This area was to become heavily populated for 180 years as a consequence of the Battle of the Diamond on 21 Sept 1795 near Loughgall, Co Armagh, Ireland, where the Protestant "Peep o' Day boys were the victors, this led to the foundation of the infamous Orange order, and the "Armagh outrages", in the North and throughout the rest of Ireland, the Catholic were by the point of the sword expelled and had to migrate, "To Hell or to Mayo". As a result, the Market Towns of East Mayo emerged, Kiltimagh, Charlestown, Kilkelly, Ballyhaunis and Swinford (aka Swineford) which became the governing town containing the Poorhouse the administration officials and the Board of Governors. Records were kept here, and maps were made of the East Mayo district.

20

RAFTERY ROOM

It's only a couple of hours to Ireland,
Where loved ones are thinking of you,
The heath it is shining,
Our hearts they are pining,
To welcome you home to old Rosin Dubh.

Come in the Springtime,
When the Shamrocks are growing,
Leave behind you the city,
The fears and the gloom.

Grand songs we'll be singing,
Half sets we'll be swinging,
At great happy nights,
In the Raftery Room.

Standing: Paddy Walsh, Archbishop Joe Cunnane, Dympna O'Reilly, John Joe Walsh and Mary O'Reilly Jerry Walsh
Sitting: Patrick O'Reilly and his father Patrick Reilly his wife Anne Winifred Morley with baby Brendan F.X. Reilly
MP Walsh his wife Celia nee Mulkeen
John Joe Walsh and Mary O'Reilly Wedding RC Kiltimagh 30 June 1947

Figure 15 Wedding of John Joe Walsh and Mary O'Reilly

THE RAFTERY ROOM

Air: The Men of the West
In song may your voices be raised,
May your stories dispel any gloom,
May the glories of Erin be praised,
When you visit the Raftery Room.

May the hand of the fiddler keep on playing,
The old tunes that never have died,
May the beat of your feet keep on saying,
Leave anger and worries outside.

May the exile heed call that has brought him,
To kneel down and pray on the sod,
And give thanks to the parents who taught him,
To walk in the image of God.

May the Reel of the young Irish maiden,
And the music of fiddle and bow,
Remind you once more of Killaiden,
Where Raftery was born long ago.

May our debt soon have paid him with justice,
By Cross, By Statue, By Tomb,
May his name and his fame be still with us,
If it's only the name of a Room.

Figure 16 Jerry Cooney from New York.
Both sets of his Grandparents came from Kiltimagh

CO ROSCOMMON 1944
ALL IRELAND CHAMPIONS

Words written Jerry Walsh, Raftery Room, Kiltimagh.

Jerry Walsh was invited by Bill Healy, Manager of the National Bank, Roscommon to produce this work. It was performed by the K.Y.M.S. (Kiltimagh Young Men's Society) Concert Troupe for the Supporters Club of County Roscommon in the Harrison Hall to a packed house at the Victory Concert on the Tuesday after the All-Ireland Final in 1944. The K.Y.M.S. Concert troupe togged out in Roscommon jerseys and togs. There were many encores and plenty of celebration to the poem composed by Jerry Walsh of the Raftery Room, Kiltimagh. Jimmy Murray from Knockcroghery captained the 1943 team, the first time that County Roscommon lifted the coveted 'Sam Maguire'. It was the beginning of a remarkable period of achievement that becomes more luminous the further into history it retreats.

Roscommon won the All-Ireland championship in 1943 and 1944, buckled in 1945 and rose again to produce what Murray believes was their best season of football before losing to Kerry in the All-Ireland final after a replay.

Roscommon's record seems a perfect example of just how difficult and elusive the ultimate prize is, for all counties other than the eternal giants of the game.

CONNAGHT FINAL 1944
ROSCOMMON V MAYO
Air: Moonlight in Mayo

'Twas up in Tuam some weeks ago Roscommon met Mayo,
The team that won the Championship not many years ago,
The crowd all came in traps and bikes, the best you've ever seen,
And McNamara's Band was togged out in the Red and Green.

The Mayo men they were willing, getting ready for the killing,
Sure, they thought they would be winning, at the whistle's final blow,
But Roscommon fairly shook them, as them frees they freely took them,
And the only thing they left them, was the Moonlight in Mayo.

Chorus: Air: McNamara's Band

His name is Jimmy Murray, the Captain of the team,
They won the cup for the second time with Ireland's best 15,
He comes from Knockcroghery, a village rather small,
Where even the goats and donkeys, now have learned to play football.

When the referee blows – the whistle it goes, – The ball goes into play,
As Murray drives the old pigskin, the fans shout "hip hurray",
Just like a flying bomb she goes, beneath the wooden beam,
A credit to all Ireland is that great Roscommon team.

Figure 17 Jimmy Murray, Captain Roscommon Team

SEMI-FINAL 1944
ROSCOMMON V CAVAN (5.8 to 2.3)

Air: Come Back Paddy Reilly

The gar- den of E- den has va- nished, they say, But I know the lie of it

Oh! Cavan, they say have a wonderful team,
Of footballers they have the cream,
They were top of the North for year after year,
This wonderful Gaelic fifteen.

But those Cavan Slashers Roscommon did slash,
With a thrashing like never-before,
So, go back Paddy Reilly to Ballyjamesduff,
And help them to tot up that score.

ALL IRELAND FINAL 1944
ROSCOMMON V KERRY

Air: The Rose of Tralee

The pale moon was ri-sing a-bove the green moun-tain The sun was de - clin-ing

Figure 18 Roscommon GAA Colours

Croke Park was crowded that day in September,
All Ireland was present the final to see,
The teams were parading, the Artane Boys were playing,
When the Blue and the Gold met the Gold and the Green,
Now, the Kingdom were out a new record to make,
Roscommon felt sure that this would not be,
They would soon show them the West was awake.
And put a Roscommon mini on the Rose of Tralee.

Figure 19 County Roscommon All Ireland Champions 1943 and 1944

Figure 20 Dermot Early County Roscommon

ALL IRELAND CHAMPIONS
ST. COLEMAN'S SENIOR TEAM

His name is Eugene Macken, he led Coleman's great fifteen,
They showed the rest of Ireland, how Gaelic football should be seen,
He told his men "to win, to win" the Hogan Cup our dream,
The champions of All Ireland are St Coleman's senior team.

With John Boyle there at centre-field – he comes from old Derrowl,
Adrian Garvey by his side, this pair would never foul,
With Carmelites attacking, centre field they could not shake,
Claremorris boys proved our joys- the West was still awake.

And then, we come to Hyland, the goalie of great fame,
James Keane from Claremorris added 2 points to the game,
Andrew Mack from Kiltimagh – we all know he's a twin,
Fed on Mack's bread and bracks - he has the speed to win.

Padraic Monaghan, Garrymore, Eddie McLoughlin, Irishtown,
Aiden Varley in defence – he comes from near Milltown,
Brave Gilmartin from Kiltimagh, Padraic Coyne star fullback,
With Michael Walsh, in red and green, repelled the Moate attack.

Cuddy's hair is curly,
but his points are curly, too,
With Declan Lambe on his line,
And McGuinness good and true,
They're a credit to St Coleman's,
To Claremorris and Mayo, too.

And now I'd say a prayer for the man behind the scene,
The man that trained this Coleman team into Ireland's best fifteen,
He broke all the records – all records smashed galore,
May the name of Fr Newell live in Coleman's evermore.

MAYO vs MEATH 1951

At Boul- a- vogue, as the sun was set- ting, O'er bright May mead- ows of

Air: Boolavogue

Jerry Walsh Kiltimagh 1951

In old Croke Park as the sun was shining,
On the football final some hours ago,
The referee's call set thousands cheering,
For royal Meath and the men of Mayo.

Captain Sean Flanagan from dear old Ballagh,
Marched up the pitch with his fourteen men,
"To win, to win, I am going to lead you,
And bring Sam Maguire to Mayo again".

With Forde and Dixon, Gilvarry, Padraic Carney,
Famous Flanagan who makes goalies shake,
Langan, Mulderrig, Wynne and John Staunton,
Have proved beyond doubt that the West is Awake.

When Eamon Mongey goes into action,
Undaunted and daring he never yields,
And Paddy Prendergast from Ballintubber,
Has downed many points on Gaelic fields.

Quinn and Irwin, and John McAndrew,
Play the game and give their best,
Where e'er they go, we always follow,
With rousing cheers for the best in the West.

God grant them glory, brave men of Mayo,
May they always play so fair and clean,
When Croke Park holds the next All Ireland,
Mayo will be there in the Red and Green.

Figure 21 Mayo All Ireland 1951 winning team Photo Courtesy of the Mayo News

Mayo 1951 All Ireland winning champions Back row L to R: James Quinn, Eugene Quinn (Brothers of Fr Peter Quinn) Paddy Jordan, Mick Loftus, John Forde, Joe Gilvarry, Tom Langan, Paddy Irwin, John McAndrew, Dr Jim Laffey (Chairman of the Mayo GAA Board) Henry Dixon, Liam Hastings, Mick Mulderrig, Gerald Courell (Trainer) Pat Conway (Treasurer Mayo GAA Board) Front L to R Willie Casey, Jackie Carney (Trainer) Sean Wynne, Mick Flanagan, Eamon Mongey, Sean Mulderrig, Fr Peter Quinn, Padraig Carney, Sean Flanagan (Capt.), Paddy Prendergast, Jimmy Curran, Joe Stanton. Photo: The Mayo News.

THE MISSIONS OF LOUIS

In 1897 on the invitation of the Parish Priest Fr Denis O'Hara six sisters of the St. Louis Order arrived from Monaghan to Kiltimagh and set up a technical school for the children of the parish, this was followed by a school for young ladies. In 1908, the school became, primarily, a boarding school for girls. The school prospered with students winning prizes on a national scale for lacemaking and proficiency in the Irish language.

Gradually, throughout the century, St. Louis Convent Secondary School, Kiltimagh, became famous throughout the country for academic and cultural endeavours. In 1973, boys enrolled in the secondary school for the first time and the boarding school was phased out. In 1992, the sisters moved out of the school and into a private residence in the town. A year later, St. Louis Secondary School amalgamated with Coláiste Rafteirí, the Vocational School, and it became known as St. Louis Community School, the St. Louis legacy remains to this day.

Ms. Max aka Peg Max from Cloughjordan, Co Tipperary was the Principal of the St louis Commercial School of Excellence for over 50 years, located on Main Street Kiltimagh where Typing, Pittman's shorthand and Book-keeping were taught to girls from all over Ireland. The course was of one to three-year duration, some girls stayed in the town in St. Louis appointed boarding houses, this helped the local economy. The trustworthy and capable graduates were much sought after, it was like a passport to work in the Ireland of tough and hard times.

The Missions of Louis

May the rosaries of all Irish mothers,
As they kneel by their firesides to pray,
Shower blessings on all our Irish missions,
In Africa, so far – far away.

May the brave Irish Sisters of Louis,
From Monaghan, Balla and Rathmines,
Be proud of that God given duty,
When soft fingers, the Rosary – entwines.

May Kiltimagh and its glory be with them,
And the teachings of Carrickmacross,
What harm if left hand is a "Kithog",
When it's making the sign of the cross.

May the breezes of bracing Bundoran,
With Ramsgate alone in the South,
Bear gently the brogue of old Erin,
And the 'Aves' to every dark mouth.

May the lessons of Dundalk and of Clogher,
Pour forth with their message serene,
Across the long road to old Shendam,
Where kind angels sing Hail Holy Queen.

May the prayers that come from old Antrim,
Ballymena and famed Cushendall,
Surmount every barrier and border,
Till the Angelus – rings over - all.

May Middleton, Newcastle and Clones,
And Kilkeel of true Irish sod,
Give daughters of Erin to Louis,
To work in the Vineyard of God.

Figure 22 St. Louis Community School

FR DENIS O'HARA

A few lines in Memory of the late Fr Denis O'Hara who died on 26 April 1922. One of his requests being that he'd be buried with his parishioners in Killicianure aka Kilkinure Graveyard outside Kiltimagh. Written by MP Walsh.

Aw brothers dear and sisters too, we're all plunged into grief,
Since God, his urgent message sent and took away our chief,
Stranger cold with heedless tread, may pass your green grave by,
But your flock in tears will visit it and pray and weep and sigh.

A faithful shepherd for fifty years, delighted with his flock,
All eyes today are chilled with tears, his death came like a shock,
Ah! Pure- sould Chief, you are not dead, from rising to setting sun,
You've done trojan work amongst us since our Priest you have become.

Figure 23 Fr Denis O'Hara P.P. Kiltimagh 1850-1922
Poem by MP Walsh circa 1923

The college stands upon the hills, o'er looks the river Glore,
Adjoins St Louis's Convent, that will stand for evermore,
As a seat of greatest learning for the brainiest and the best,
The scholars who graduated there, are a credit to the West.

The landlord shook at our Sagart's voice, the tenant emancipated,
He is now lord of his own demesne -the evicted he re-instated,
All you who're here for a few years more, forget not the kind and true,
Prayers more welcome than golden store, that's all he expects from you.

Farewell, Father Denis – a last farewell -on earth we'll meet no more!
We hope to meet in Heaven above, when earthly trials are o'er,
A faithful patriot for native land, a friend of lowly and poor,
May mother earth rest lightly o'er, your bier in Killicianure.

Figure 24 Jerry, Paddy, John Joe, MP Walsh

MELBOURNE

On the banks of gentle Yarra,
Near Mount Dandelong,
This Garden City, Melbourne,
Forever calls me on.

To say farewell to Ireland,
Four years in a row,
And leave behind dear Kiltimagh.
In the County of Mayo.

Old age it seems to leave me,
When I meet my kith and kin,
In the words of famous Raftery,
I become young – once again.

To climb once more Mount Macedon,
Noble monument in the sky,
And see historic Ballarat,
Where Eureka diggers lie.

Thank you -Mighty Melbourne,
No Stress – No Strain – No Strife,
For an Everest of a holiday,
In the evening of my life.

Figure 25 Sky High Mount Dandelong, Melbourne, Australia

A TRIBUTE TO JERRY WALSH

Terence Flanagan, Cloonfallagh, Aghamore, County Mayo 17 Jan 1999

When mighty Melbourne wins your heart,
And draws you far from here,
We celebrate your new – found youth,
With friends and daughter dear.

We know that Erin's still your home,
The native land you pride,
Yet now you trace our exiles' steps,
To where they lived and died.

We think of all your exploits here,
In noble word and deed,
For Kiltimagh and old Mayo,
And for your friends in need.

Your warm welcome brings delight,
To all who come along,
To savour life in your home - town,
With music, dance and song.

You have hosted many a famous guest,
From places far and near,
Your history and your anecdotes,
Have added to the cheer.

Your voice rings out across the globe,
On radio, tape and show,
You spread the folklore of the west,
And proudly praise Mayo.

Despite the ups and downs of life,
And all your eighty years,
You journey on in gallant style,
Inspiring all you peers

We wish you joyful days ahead,
Free from all strife and gloom,
But hope to meet you soon again,
In your famed Raftery Room.

Figure 26 Jerry Walsh Portrait

PJ MURTAGH RIP

Goodbye to my good friend PJ,
My Comrade of 65 years,
In all kinds of weather together,
Of Music, of Song and of Tears.

It is lonely today by Yarra Ranges,
Sad and dark clouds keep flying by,
Golden memories of PJ never changes,
With sorrow, I bid him goodbye.

To have my dear friend beside me,
As the end of life's journey is nigh,
A great song of his – seems to guide me,
To that long lost 'Gold mine in the sky'.

In memory of my good friend PJ Murtagh
Written by Jerry Walsh. Melbourne.

**Figure 27 PJ and Sheila Murtagh nee Mulkeen with
their Family in James St Kiltimagh circa 1960**

IRELAND A NATION AGAIN

There are six famous counties in Ireland,
With a history so glorious and grand,
Where natures wild beauty is ravished,
And the Irish Tricolour is banned.

On the Border you'll see the B. Specials,
Who have let down our own 32,
They have hate in their hearts for old Ireland,
Where once marched the men of Red Hugh.

They have set up their own iron curtain,
On the soil from which patriots came,
But the sun that shines down from the heavens,
Will forever shine down on their name.

The name of Woulfe Tone and of Casement,
Who died for our freedom to gain,
Let us strike the last blow for old Ireland,
And make her a Nation again.

We shall march up that pathway of glory,
Now lined with memories so green,
Of Pearce, of Clarke and of Plunkett,
And their comrades of 1916.

We shall follow the footsteps of Fenians,
And prove that they died not in vain,
When we fight for the freedom of Ireland,
And make her a Nation again.

Figure 28 Jeremiah O'Donovan Rossa 1831- 1915

At the grave of O'Donovan Rossa,
We shall halt there to kneel and bow,
Where the soil is caressed by the mighty,
We'll renew there our Fenian vow.

To continue the fight for our freedom,
To see that no tyrants shall reign,
To win back our own six lost counties,
And make Ireland a Nation again.

So, away with the Black and Tan Specials,
Make sure that no Paisleys remain,
Sure, we will hang out our Bunting on Bogside,
And make Ireland a Nation again.

AIRPORT IN MAYO

At Barnacogue, 12.3 miles from Knock Shrine, County Mayo, Ireland the most outlandish of dreams became a reality all thanks to a visionary cleric who wouldn't take no for an answer and who described himself as "an old man in a hurry". Charles Haughey T.D. agreed to an airport in Knock over dinner with Monsignor Horan, guaranteeing the colourful cleric, "We'll give it sympathetic consideration". That was good enough for Monsignor Horan, though the story goes that Haughey thought he had agreed to a grass strip, and the priest led the charge cleverly using the political upheaval of the early 1980s to entice support from rival political parties. With no firm commitment given, Monsignor Horan went full steam ahead, hiring workers to flatten a 7,000m strip for the runway. The airport opened on 25 October 1985 with three Aer Lingus charter flights to Rome: the official opening was on 30 May 1986. The official name for the airport is IWAK aka Ireland West Airport Knock.

IN THE SHADOW OF GREATNESS
Jimmy Horan, nephew of Monsignor James Horan; Barry Linnane, sculptor of the bronze statue; Noel Jennings, organising committee; Frank Harrington, Harrington's Quarries and Joe Gilmore, Managing Director, Ireland West Airport Knock, pictured at the unveiling of the sculpture.

Figure 29 Monsignor Horan,
Image Courtesy of Carmel Williams. Mayo News 7
May 2013.

This poem was found among Jerry's collection. It is about the Airport at Knock. Author is unknown, but its style is similar to the style of Jerry Walsh.

It's just a year ago today we started on the site,
We worked so hard, machines and men, we worked by day and night,
We moved the hill, we cleared the glen with spirits all aglow,
We made the base, we have a case for our Airport in Mayo.

We confounded all the critics who said "ye are going too far",
Saying "it can't be done, it won't be done, ye will never see it tarred",
But our gallant band under Monsignor's hand ready to have a go,
Upset the odds, the jeers and cods, for an Airport in Mayo.

For far too long, the same sing song, the West is no good at all,
But the West is awake, with a mighty quake, calling her children all,
From New York town to Epsom Downs, from Sidney to Idaho,
We'll fly you here, in another year, to our Airport in Mayo.

We call on all both great and small, to help our country's sake,
Connaught is out of her slumber now, the West is truly awake,
And Mary serene in her Celestial scene, who came to us long ago,
Will be our guiding light for every flight to our Airport in Mayo.

Figure 30 Airbus A380 land at Knock

THE O'HORA'S FROM MAYO

Jerry Walsh composed this next poem on the 5th of July 1958 for the occasion of Paddy O'Hora's wedding in Galway, Jerry Walsh's mother was Mary Ellen Walsh nee O'Hora. Mary Ellen's niece Kay O'Hora was married to William O'Hora the Film censor, and he was the brother of Paddy O'Hora mentioned above and related to the "bone setter" Paddy O'Hora family.
The Family of James O'Hora 1878-1942 came from Treenagleragh,

You've heard of many famous men from around Kill-time-town,
They are scattered all around the world in cities of renown,
They have made their name from deeds of fame,
as champions they were born,
a credit to old Ireland were the men from old Slieve Horn.

Figure 31 Spanker's Hill

And high upon that gallant list of famous Irishmen,
Are the O'Hora's from Treenagleragh, boys, Louis, Joe and Vin,
They left their mark in England and in Africa far away,
And now we hear they are marching on the grand old USA.

With Francis at the farming in those Irish fields so green,
He'll keep the home flag flying there, the best you've ever seen,
Father Aiden in the Mission field, with courage staunch and true,
He's a credit to Kill-time-agh, and to God and Ireland too.

We have Kathleen here as Matron, to nurse our aches and pains,
Sure, Margaret might follow in the steps of Sister James,
Or start a home like Nazareth-like her Mother long ago,
That Queen of Irish Mothers-Mrs O'Hora from Mayo.

And now we're going to drink a toast on Paddy's wedding day,
An Honour of the McNulty Clan-and those who are far away,
We wish good luck to Teresa – God's blessings with her stay,
May Heaven bless your wedding here on the shores of Galway Bay.

Air: McNamara's Band

Figure 32 Vincent O'Hora, Kiltimagh. Mayo 1951 Supporter
Photo courtesy of Keith Heneghan Photography.

BON SECOURS OUT RENMORE WAY

If you e- ver go a- cross the sea to Ire- land,

Sure, it's maybe some-day I'll go back to Galway,
If it's only for a week or for a day,
To be nursed again by friendly nurses,
In famous Bon Secours out Renmore way.

Dr. Duffy - successful and so caring.
As he keeps a watchful eye right all over,
Which he got as a boy – a seafaring,
On that lovely Isle off Donegal.

Dr. Garvey gives your ears a mighty tingle,
Mr Comer helps you see things far and near,
Dr. Bresnihan's ultrasound - from old Dingle,
Echoes daddy's memories from Castlebar.

The brave man – John Nee from Connemara,
Has sent happy people on their way,
With a hand as famed as the Hill of Tara,
As he works beside his own dear Galway Bay.

Thank you, Dr. Lang, for your attention,
I am happy forever to now record,
Your assistance in my search of a lifetime,
You have helped me find that famous old lost chord!.

Continue the great welcome at reception,
Congratulations to your masters of X ray,
Thank you to all the staff during my time,
In famous Bon Secours down Renmore way.

SEAN'S 50TH BIRTHDAY

We send you greetings from Melbourne,
To Seán on his fiftieth Birthday,
From Dad, Celia, Alan and Ivan,
On this most wonderful day.

Our thoughts are with you so often,
Although we are so far away,
You are loved and not forgotten,
As you reach fifty years old, to-day,

It brings back many memories,
Of that morning long – ago,
When Mammy cried out for help,
"Get moving – don't be slow".

Aunt Bea came on duty,
That big smile on her face,
With her uniform of beauty,
And her medals all in place.

And when I tried to help her,
She made all things very clear,
"Come back in the evening time".
"You have caused all this trouble here".

Thank you, Mary Ellen,
For minding Sean so well,
You removed the fears down all these years,
Of Cara, of Digital and of Nortel.

With Darragh on the Rugby,
Anton, hurling keen,
Deirdre – a fine Nurse will be,
The finest ever seen.

May your years be full of happiness,
Of good health, of work and of play,
As you march into the next fifty,
Down Ballindooley way.

Jerry was in Melbourne when he wrote this poem with the conclusion
"Love Pop 27 March 2000

Figure 33 Bea Gormally May 1954 with Jer Walsh

Back Row L to R: Midwife Bea Gormally holding Jer Walsh.
Centre: Jerry and Kay Walsh nee Conlon.
Front Row L to R: Sean, Celia, and Paddy.
May 1954 Corner House Kiltimagh.

Affectionately known as Aunt Bea aka Bridget Agnes Gormally 1897-1985
was born in Cloondoolagh, Kiltimagh, she was the District Nurse and
Midwife who delivered Seán Walsh on the 27 March 1950 in James Street,
Kiltimagh where his parents Jerry and Kay Walsh nee Conlon from Mount
Town, Killadoon, Geevagh Parish, County Sligo, Ireland were living. Aunt
Bea a good friend of the Walsh Family and an Aunt to John Joe Walsh's wife
Mary O'Reilly, Bea was married to James Gormally they had three children
Margaret Mary (Poem included), Seán and Marcella who married John Forde
(Poem included). Seán Walsh is married to a Midwife Mary Ellen Howlan
from County Wexford, they have three children Darragh, Anton and Dierdre.

FAMILY OF JERRY WALSH

Figure 34 Family of Jerry Walsh

FRANCIS COLGAN
MARCHES ON

Air: McNamara's Band
Words: Jerry Walsh circa 1961

You've heard of Thomas Lipton, and his chain shops of the Crown,
and all the other Loyalists, from Woolworths limited down,
How they opened shops all over, from Dublin to Mayo,
To Britain and the Empire, all the profits they did go.

Then at last it took a rebel, their loyal hearts to break,
To show the rest of Ireland, that the West is still Awake,
A soldier true of '22, when freedom was being won,
He certainly showed the "Mausteens" how big business could be done.

Chorus: McNamara's Band

His name is Francis Colgan, he comes from Carragowan,
Adjacent to Bohola, in that famous seaport town,
The home of many heroes, in story and in song,
Undaunted and successful, Francis Colgan marches on.

Figure 35 Kilkelly Monument 4 June 1877
James Groarke, Frank Colgan, General Tom Barry
(Who did the unveiling), John Snee

It started in Rialto, not so many years ago,
With black hens' eggs from Coilltemagh, he made that business grow,
He opened branches here and there, the best you've ever seen,
And then we heard he landed in, home markets on the Green.

And then he marched on Crumlin, where the yellow house once stood,
Under Tommy Dwan's watchful eye, the porter it was good,
Sure, the Guinness flows like beestings, and they come from near and far,
To have good cheer and Smithwick's beer, in Colgan's County Bar.

Figure 36 Frank Colgan's famous white champion
who won many prizes at shows in England on his
exhibition 26 March 1952 20 cwts 7 lbs price £120

Figure 37 Lucan Spa Hotel Dublin

With Ballyfermot next in line, he soon picked out his stand,
He built a Pub, and Lounge Bar there, the finest in the land,
For those thousands of hard-working men, they had no place to sup,
It gave them delight, to queue at night, in the Ballyfermot Pub.

Having conquered all the outskirts, without suffering one defeat,
He moved into the centre of, busy Parliament Street,
The Corporations worried, and so are Fianna Fail,
The Bohola guy has got his eye, on Dublin's City Hall.

And then he found that Dublin, sure it wasn't big enough,
He bought the Lucan Spa Hotel, he will make it do its stuff,
For Colleens fair, of beauty rare, to the West he'll have to go,
The only thing he'll leave us there, is the Moonlight in Mayo.

And now I'm going to tell you, the cause of Frank's success,
It's the brains behind the curtain, of our charming new hostess?
With their nine young handsome children, (I think they will need sixteen),
We wish them luck, this opening night, 'neath the orange, white and green.

Now to finish with my chorus, I wish you lots of joy,
I hope that you'll be happy here, with our fine Bohola Boy,
There's a hearty "Céad Míle Fáilte" here,
from Colgan from Mayo.

Figure 38 Linda Colgan, Cassie Canning, Frank Colgan. Gerald Colgan

GRAND FAREWELL SOCIAL OLD TOWN HALL

Words: by Jerry Walsh

The old Town Hall is finished,
Its days of life are few,
It proudly takes historic place,
And makes way for the new.

It brings back happy memories,
Of Plays and Concerts grand,
Of Drama, and of Dances,
The finest in the Land.

And now before it closes down,
Let us have a final date,
At a farewell dance by Tidy Town,
Before it is too late.

Cause it's going to be a factory,
Spinning night and noon and morn,
To keep our youth in Ireland,
In the place where they were born.

Pete Brown's Showband
Grand get-together for young and old
Tues Jan 25th
ADM. 4/- Dancing 9 pm

Western People 12 December 2001 Michael Commins reported that
Kiltimagh and showbiz friends bid farewell to Pete Browne from
Kiltimagh, a prominent bandleader of the show band era. Pete died recently
at his home in Chapel Street, Kiltimagh.

**Figure 39 Pete Browne Showband Tooreen 1958 photo courtesy of
Basil Burke**

News of his passing saddened his many friends in the music business throughout the area who had known him as a man dedicated to his love of music over the years and to keeping the highest of standards, whilst on the stage. Pete had a love for music since his early years.

The advent of the show band era with the arrival of the Clipper Carlton Show Band from Tyrone, heralded a sea-change in the Irish entertainment scene. At the other end of the country, the Royal Show band came swash-buckling out of Waterford. It was the era when Ireland was swinging to the sounds of the big show bands. The bands mushroomed in towns and villages all over the country. It became a huge industry giving employment to an estimated 6,000 people at its peak. In Kiltimagh, Pete Browne was making his own plans. His Band of Renown soon became popular favourites on the western circuit and in many parts of Donegal.

A talented band with a strong brass section specialising in the popular music of the day. (In later years Pete called his band the Sundowners).

In 1962, Pete Browne and his Band of Renown became the sixth Irish show band to fly the Atlantic and take in a tour of American cities. It was the first of a number of such ventures that saw the Kiltimagh based band strike a rich vein in the hearts of the western exiles. Speaking to Michael Commins sometime ago, Pete recalled their first trip to New York after jetting out from Shannon Airport. "People began to queue outside the famous City Centre Ballroom in Manhattan a few hours before we were due on stage".

At that time, the idea of an Irish show band traveling to America was still new, only five had gone before us including the Royal, the Capitol and the Johnny Flynn Show band from Tuam. "We also played to huge crowds in Chicago, Cleveland and the New State Ballroom in Boston". Numerous people remarked about Pete's wonderful voice and delivery. It was quite exceptional. Pete's band that toured America included Doc Carroll, Brian Carr, with Frank and Vincent Gill, all of whom later went on to form the Royal Blues Show band, as well as Pete's brother James. James died last year in Kiltormer, County Galway, and the late Billy Holian from Tuam. Doc Carroll then became the first singer from Connacht to register a Number One in the Irish Top 20 with Old Man Trouble.

Figure 40 MP and Celia Walsh and Family circa 1930

FAREWELL TO ROBYN

Sure, its maybe she'll come back to see us,
If it's only for an hour or for a day,
To greet everyone – at 201,
And grace again our own Boronia way.

To see again our own dear teacher, Robyn,
Whose "Yop Chugi" would chase your foes away,
With "Dolio Chugi", "Kisson" and gracious "Kanye",
Sure - Robyn brought us all Taekwondo way.

It's a long way from Scoresby Road to Queensland,
Our loss is Surfers Paradise's gain,
We will miss our own great teacher, Robyn,
And she returns to Melbourne soon again.

May your days be full of contentment,
And your 'Mom' remains mighty I pray,
May your style be forever with you,
Is the wish of your friends in Boronia way.

Figure 41 Jerry Walsh circa 1948

BERNIE AND TONY

Greetings to lovely Bernie and Tony,
On their Ruby Anniversary Day,
May God's choicest blessing be ever with you,
And guide you in a very special way.

It brings back many fond memories,
When Carrowbehy joined Ballinamore,
And Bod Crawley brought me up to Dublin,
In my teenage happy years of yore.

At 85 – my travelling is now over,
And the amber will soon shine up high,
Fond memories of Bod and young Tim,
Will be with me till I say goodbye.

Jerry Walsh Kiltimagh 2003

BILL McKELVEY

No more we'll meet that mighty man,
From Donegal he came,
The finest of great Irishmen,
Bill McKelvey is his name.

With Mary from Roscommon,
And Bill from Donegal,
They were known all over Melbourne,
And the finest couple of them all.

The door was always open,
To welcome someone's son,
When calling here from Ireland,
At Victoria's Number one.

Its lonely round Hotel Bayswater,
Where memories of Bill will never die,
His pals around him in a ring,
The stories he would bring,
He showed us how to live,
Then he showed us how to die.

Farewell, to my friends Bill and Mary,
May God's blessings never fail,
To guard you there forever,
In historic Lilydale.

With golden memories of Bill and Mary
Jerry Walsh
Kiltimagh

TO VINCE AND MARILYN

May your house be 'piles' with contentment,
And your days full of happiness serene,
May your love be forever cemented,
Since Vince made Marilyn his Queen.

It's a long way from Knock to Port Hedland,
The Congo and Snowy Mountain scheme,
You have both slept in this 'Bedland',
And no pony or trap to be seen.

Farewell to you both from old Jerry,
As I travel to old road to Slieve Horn,
When we meet again, we'll be merry,
In old Ireland, where great men are born.

**Figure 42 Kiltimagh 1925 John Joe aged 8, Jerry aged 7,
and Paddy Walsh aged 10.**

KATIE CASBY MULKEEN

May your days be full of contentment,
And your nineties full of happiness serene,
From Celia and Jerry in Melbourne,
To our dear friend – Katie Casby-Mulkeen.

Killarney circa 1960
Katie Casby nee Mulkeen N.T., Kay Walsh nee Conlon, The Jarvey, and
Jerry Walsh, Raftery Room.

Figure 43 Katie Casby, Kay Walsh, Jerry Walsh

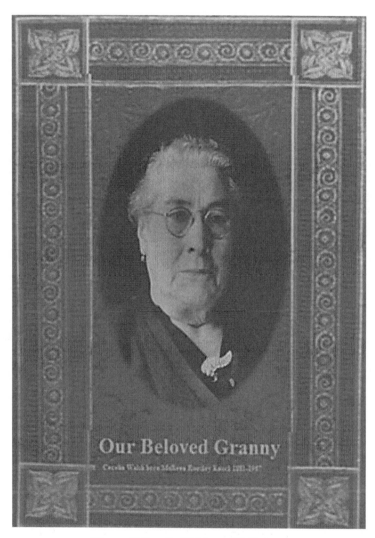

Figure 44 Cecelia Walsh nee Mulkeen

HAPPY BIRTHDAY TO CELIA

Figure 45 photo courtesy of Maureen O'Brien

Happy Birthday to Celia,
Happy Birthday to you,
Greetings from Alan and Ivan,
And from your Daddy too.

Sean

My six months here in Melbourne,
Were really really great,
To enjoy your lovely birthday,
In dear old Mountain Gate.

Paddy

It brings back fondest memories,
Of 46 years ago,
When you landed in 'St Anne's,
Blue eyes and cheeks aglow.

Jer

Thank you for your welcome,
It's hard to say goodbye,
When leaving Mighty Melbourne,
I am trying not to cry.

Pierce

I want you to remember,
As Qantas takes to the sky,
You'll see the white flag waving,
As Daddy says goodbye.

Barry

God bless you darling Celia,
Alan and Ivan know,
To win Cricket on the Wicket,
And black belt Taekwondo.

Nathy

I am dreaming of November,
As the sky I fly across,
To greet my dearest Celia,
'Neath the stars of the Southern Cross.

Damien

Well, Jerry and Margaret would you believe,
A Walsh and a Carney they did conceive,
Our Tony, a Brady,
It's just now we did find,
With Tom Jordan and Fran!
Can This world be more kind?

Tony

Melbourne 10 November 1998
Love Daddy, Alan, and Ivan

Figure 46 Alan Jerry and Ivan

MAFIA MAM

Grand memories of old Treenagleragh,
Great parties of beer and of ham,
Have now moved down here, to Melbourne,
To honour our own Mafia Mam.

When Annie played the accordion,
And John took the floor in a reel,
The music flowed down Treenagleragh,
Could be heard as far as – Treenkeel.

Those days are gone forever,
No dances no reels on the hill,
But the spirit of John and of Annie,
Forever will play in Boxhill.

As Michael goes back to old Coillte,
Where all the Roache history began,
And old Jerry returns to great Melbourne,
To meet Celia – and our own Mafia Mam.

There's a rumour floating 'round us,
Only lately did I hear,
Of Irish matchmaking,
Of Jerry and Betty dear.

But when you come to eighty,
In life's race I also ran,
Betty is still my favourite,
God bless you – Mafia Mam.

And now it's time to say goodbye,
For words, I'm at a loss,
Thank you Betty, and the Roache's,
In the land of the Southern Cross.

ANNIE MAY AND JOHNNY KELLY

Greeting to Annie May and Johnny,
As golden fifty years come along,
Best wishes from Celia and Jerry,
From the foothills of grand Dandelong.

It is many a road you have travelled,
Many a call you did fill,
One call, the call of a lifetime,
Annie May from lovely Thornhill.

When we heard the sirens wailing,
Olden banshee made us afraid,
'Twas Kelly's men across the glen,
With Kiltimagh fire brigade.

May the road ahead treat you kindly,
And traffic lights forever shine green,
It is the wish of great friends around you,
Many miles of happiness serene.

Drive on with your mountain of memories,
Of happiness around Pollagh and Glore,
Your full load of history and stories,
Bring joy and laughter galore.

Figure 47 Annie May and Johnny Kelly, Aiden St.

BETTY - QUEEN OF THE CLAN

Greetings to Betty this evening,
May golden memories ever survive,
On this very happy occasion,
On your Birthday today, February five.

Annie's music comes from Treenagleragh,
Sure, it echoes around Boxhill,
When John danced a reel in the kitchen,
At the foot of old Spanker's Hill,

Grand memories of mighty Manchester,
Forever they seem to come back,
Where Betty fell in love with the Roaches,
And married their wonderful Jack.

We enjoyed your visit to Ireland,
Shamrock Travel will bring you back soon,
As the grand twins do Irish dancing,
To the cheers in the Raftery Room.

May your years be full of contentment,
And your days filled with happiness serene,
With your Children and Grandchildren around you,
They all love you, Betty the Queen.

Figure 48 Treenagleragh Kiltimagh

THE FAHEYS FROM SUNBURY

We salute the Fahey's from Sunbury,
Where real Irish welcomes are made,
Christine, Greg and Joanna,
With their lovely princess, called Sinead.

To meet again brave – Tim Fahey,
Whose faith is like Cashel Rock,
He has knelt at Lourdes and at Fatima,
And prays at the grand Shrine at Knock.

Great memories of dear Jim and Lucy,
As the young Sligo couple next door,
Join Vicenta, Lita and Mattie,
With singing and music galore.

At the 'Red Rose Cafe' in the cellar,
Beer, Wine and Guinness stacked so high,
We hear Greg's voice a-singing,
"It's lonely round the Fields of Athenry",

We remember Old Emo Bottom,
As Mount Macedon reaches the sky,
Ballarat is never forgotten,
Where brave Eureka Diggers lie.

March on – GOOD MAN – TIM FAHEY,
It's a long way to Tipperary's green sod,
Sure, the Angels in Heaven,
To help in the Vineyard of God.

With Compliments of Jerry Walsh, Melbourne

PADDY HIGGINS 80TH BIRTHDAY

May your days be full of contentment,
Higgin's Coatings will banish all fears,
Is the wish of the Walsh's in Ireland,
On your Birthday of grand 80 years.

It's a long way Bohola to Bambooka,
From Rathslevin so peaceful and green,
To Doncaster where traffic is faster,
Than the high road to old Toor-o-meen.

I'm glad to be here with my Celia,
On Paddy's great 80th Birthday,
With mountains of memories back with me,
As I drive down Rathslevin Way.

We salute the Clan of Higgins,
Tonight, in historic Kooyong,
Undaunted and successful,
Paddy Higgins – marches on.

**Figure 49 Higgins Family
Maureen, Paddy. Helen**

**Figure 50 Peter, Martin,
Gerry, John, Paddy.**

WAITING FOR THE POSTMAN

By Jerry Walsh 1970

Each morning we ask of each other,
"Has the postman a letter today"?
From Paddy the Piper, our loved one,
From the shores of Amerikay.

Each night we just keep on saying,
"New York's just like, a Coillte Fair Day,
The young lad has no time for writing,
All we can do here, is pray".

We pray for the good friends beside him,
And keep him on the right path each day,
Sure, we know we can never forget them,
And hope to repay them some day.

It's lonely today in Old Ireland,
When Postman Miko delivers his round,
His bag is as light as a stripper,
That John Forde could buy for a pound.

We know you are up in the morning,
Joe Nestor, he gives you the knock,
And Margaret says, bed, without warning,
When the time comes 'round Ten O'clock.

Give our regards to Frank and to Agnes,
Our own Tess, the boys, Annie May,
Tell Tilly, Chris, and Jim Benson,
That Sniper is cutting the hay.

Pake Murtagh still guards old Cloondoolagh,
As he marches each day on his round,
Tom George directs traffic at Pollagh,
Sure! no better cop could be found.

We hope you will keep the flag flying,
Undaunted - Undaring - Unafraid,
When you play the Pipes along Broadway,
In the City your forefathers made.

And when it comes to the evening,
"Will you sit down and drop us a line,
To the father that worked hard to rear you,
And that grand Irish Mother of thine".

Figure 51 St Patrick's Day parade, New York. 17 March
1970 Photo courtesy of Jim Benson, Kiltimagh.

FORTY PUBS SO CLEAN

I close my eyes and picture,
The dust going down the street,
From the road that leads to Pollagh,
To the end of Aiden Street.

I miss the grand old Navvy,
With her music so serene,
It sounded like a showband,
Playing Forty Shades of Green.

Chorus

But most of all I miss Staball,
In dear old Culchie town,
And most of all, I can't recall,
Where the road went up and down.

Again, I want to write and sing,
Of the things that should have been,
And sing old songs of Kiltimagh,
Where we never knew 'Christine'.

I'd love to send those Engineers,
To Comderra's lovely turf,
I'd love to watch the Ganger, too,
Spade the bog and foot the turf.

And then I'd bring the Farmers in,
From their meadows bright and green,
To down that dust with an Irish thirst,
In our forty pubs so clean.

Written by Jerry Walsh (The town was upside down during the installation
of the new sewage scheme)

HAPPY BIRTHDAY NURSE KATHLEEN

Happy Birthday dear Kathleen,
Happy Birthday to you,
Greetings from Clare to Mayo,
And from Arizona, too.

It brings back happy memories,
That will last for evermore,
Of the Kelly's from Treenkeel,
On the banks of the River Glore.

Thank you, great Nurse Kathleen,
For your gentle nursing - cares,
When you taught me how to walk again!
Up and down Galvia Stairs.

We have heard all about you,
Good works you cannot conceal,
Around County Clare and Kilmurray,
Of Kathleen from Treenkeel.

You are welcome here from Phoenix,
And from Ohio, too,
Dublin, Manchester and County Clare,
With greetings fond and true.

To our own dear Nurse, Kathleen,
It's time to dance a reel,
Or sing a Happy Birthday,
To Kathleen, from Treenkeel.

PATRICK DERMOT BRENNAN

Jerry Walsh replied to a letter in 1944 from Patrick Dermot Brennan in the United States whose family came from Greyfield, Kiltimagh. The following lines were included, and the author is unknown.

At the Oxford Bridge mating,
The Greyfield's are waiting,
The Gaffe it is shining,
Like never before,
The extra half gallon,
Will account for more Salmon,
That never again,
Will come up by the Glore.

Figure 52 Patrick Dermot Brennan

TO MARGARET ON HER 80TH BIRTHDAY

Margaret Gormally of Aiden St 1924-2005 was married to Eddie O'Hagan from Churchtown, Dublin. She played an active part in KYMS. Her children were Pat and Michelle.

May your days be full of contentment,
And coming years banish all fears,
Is the wish of your friends in old Coillte,
On your birthday of grand 80 years.

It's a long road dear Margaret you've travelled,
Since Eddie – that great man you did meet,
When you stole away the beauty of our town,
The Queen of our Aiden Street.

I treasure great memories of old days,
When St louis uniform you wore,
You were star of drama and great plays,
We thought those days would last evermore.

Keep the O'Hagan flag flying,
As the eighties now roll along,
Dear Margaret is forever remembered,
In history – in word – and in song.

May the road ahead guide you safely,
And bright lights forever shine down,
On the love of Pat, of George and Michelle,
And on Margaret – the heart of Churchtown.

From Jerry
The Friend of a Lifetime

LIBERTY'S SWORD

Poem written by MP aka Mike Patsy Walsh the father of Jerry Walsh.

I love the bright sword of the fearless and brave,
It's that weapon that ever gives life to the slave,
How glorious it glitters through liberty's fight,
As it strikes down the hireling arranged against right.

As it cleaves through the helmet and pierces the shield,
And fells the oppressor in that blood-tinged field,
It is rendered historic before tyranny's horde,
But retreat must flash before Liberty's sword.

There is grandeur sublime in its magical stroke,
And thrones are upturned, and sceptres are broke,
Of loyal upholders of slaves of the sod,
As the free man stands up in the image of God.

As leaves in October fall off. their tall trees,
All are swept away. by the swift passing breeze,
And idols which despots, had fondly adored,
Are shattered to Earth, by the might of the sword.

Though experienced politicians, again and again,
Describe as all-powerful, the voice and the pen,
Though pseudo philosophers, and Gilbeys might preach,
Yet the lesson of manhood, they cannot unteach.

For still 'tis a maxim, deny it who may,
It's as clear as the noontide, of midsummer day,
That never a Nation, got freedom restored,
Until flashed and demanded, with the point of the Sword.

There is a lesson in this, on which all may depend,
That the Warriors' sword, is humanity's friend,
And that he won't yield it, has slavery's brand,
For freedom dwells in, that steel guarded hand.

She takes her abode, with the soldier of right,
With arms to combat, oppression and might,
When memories will cherish, its ill-gotten horde,
Then freedom will cling, to the man of the sword.

Then. here's to the brave Irish hero,
Who loves but the true and the brave!
And has sworn to free, his loved country,
Or perish, in Liberty's grave.

Hurrah, to the brave Irish colleen,
Who refuses to part, with her hand!
To the buachaill, who has not got the courage,
To fight for his down – trodden land.

Figure 53 MP Walsh Corner house Kiltimagh

FR JOSEPH WALSH

Kiltimagh-Perth
The last Priest to leave Ireland for Australia 1976

Welcome - Fr Joe to Ireland,
From the City of Light, lovely Perth,
25 years away, from your homeland,
Welcome back, to the land of your birth.

Thank you, Mike Byrne, and – Dear Dua,
Eoin, Donnacha and Deirdre so fine,
Happy days, by the Indian Ocean,
Bring memories, of Grand Currimbine.

We salute C, Y. O'Connor – Mundaring,
Paddy Hannon – Kalgoorlie – First Gold,
John Boyle O'Reilly's escape – Freemantle,
And his comrades – the Fenians of old.

Farewell Fr Joe – Nollnamara,
Parishioners proudly helped you each day,
To bring on the glory of Tara,
To Our Lady of Lourdes, Marda Way.

As we view Subiaco Gardens,
The Common, Station Clock and the Lake,
Market Square Park and the Fountains,
Show the world that Perth is awake.

Lead on - Fr Joe in Subiaco,
With vision and Irish talent galore,
With your plans – Number one Salvado,
And St Joseph's will last evermore.

With the compliments of Jerry Walsh

CLASS OF 1925 ST LOUIS NS KILTIMAGH

Figure 54 Boys and girls Kiltimagh 1925

NAMES OF CLASS OF 1925

1925 or 1926		Newtownbrowne NS			Kiltimagh Co Mayo				Please complete and correct			Paddy Walsh	
		or St Louis National School			Ireland		57 Pupils					James St	
												862310593	
BOYS													
Front Row			1	2	3	4,"X"	5	6	7	8			
L to R			Brennan	John	John	Joe	Fr Louis	Eamon	"D"	Seamus			
			Cortoon	Gates	Murrell	Quinn	Madden	Jordan	Higgins	Burke			
			Canbrack	Thos St	Aiden St		James St	James St	Kilcon	Aiden St			
2nd Row		1	2	3	4	5	6	7	8	9	10		
L to R		Jack	"D"	Jim	Con	Tom	Andy	John Joe	Tom		Vinny		
		Higgins	Murtagh	Begley	Jordan	Forde	Runane	Walsh	Garvey		Kelly		
		Thos St	Hibernian	Aiden St	Aiden St	Chaple St	Main St	Main St	Aiden St		Thomas St		
		Bank											
Back Row	1	2	3	4	5	6	7	8	9	10	11	12	13
L to R			Conneely		Michael	Charlie	Jimmy	Henry	Jerry	Tom	Eugene	Kieran	Vincent
			Upper		Murtagh	O'Neill	Dempsey	Jordan	Walsh	Runane	Kilduff	McHugh	Murtagh
			Main St		Aiden St	Cordarragh		Aiden St	Main St	Main St	Thos St	Thomas St	Hib. Bank
GIRLS	1	2	3 and 4	5	6	7	8	9	10	11	12	13	14
Front Row							Eta		Madilene	Magery	Ita		Ann May
L to R		Loftus					Murtagh	Brennan	Rowan	Carroll	McHugh		Coyle
		Chaple St		Brennan			C.Kedagh	C.Doolagh	James St	St louis	Chaple St		Main St
				Coocahore									
2nd Row	1	2	3	4	5	6	7	8	9	10	11	12	13
L to R							Maud	Tessie	Aine		Katie	Micta	
				Iver			Rowan	McNicholas	Murphy	Freeley	Carroll	Loftus	
				Coocahore			James St		Main St	Poolagh	Cordarr-	Thomas St	
										Mill D's	agh		
										Mary Jo			
										Brennan			

Figure 55 Names of Pupils Class of 1925

JERRY'S SING ALONG

With the compliments of Jerry Walsh

The role of Master of Ceremonies was perfect job for Jerry Walsh from a young age on the stage to introduce an Act, a Play, a Drama, a Dance, or just to say a few words. This sing-along was developed and evolved during WW2 when the light and the food was scarce, and the nights were long.

Rosie O Grady.

Sweet Rosie O'Grady, my beautiful Rose,
She's my beautiful lady, that everyone knows,
And when we are married how happy we'll be,
For I love sweet Rosie O'Grady,
And Rosie O'Grady loves me.

I'll be your sweetheart.

I'll be your sweetheart, if you will be mine,
All my life I'll be your Valentine,
Blue bells will gather, keep them and be true,
When I'm a man my plan will be to marry you.

Now is the hour.

Now is the hour when we must say goodbye,
Soon you will be sailing far across the sea,
When you are away oh! Please remember me,
When you return, you'll find me waiting here.

It's a long way to Tipperary.

It's a long way to Tipperary, It's a long way to go,
It's a long way to Tipperary, to the sweetest girl I know,
Goodbye Piccadilly, farewell Leicester Square.
It's a long-long way to Tipperary, but my heart's right there.

Keep right on to the end of the road.

Keep right on to the end of the road,
keep right on to the end,
Though the way be long, let your heart be strong,
Keep right on round the bend.

Though you are tired and weary still journey on,
Till you come to your happy abode,
When all you love, you've been dreaming on,
Will be there at the end of the road.

Wild Rover.

I've been a wild rover for many a year,
And I've spent all my money on whiskey and beer,
But now I'm returning with gold in great store,
And I'll never will play the wild rover no more.
And it's no nay never, no nay never no more,
Will I play the wild rover, no never no-more!

These are my mountains.

For fame and for fortune I've wandered the earth,
But now I've returned to the land of my birth,
I've brought back my treasures but only to find,
They are less than the treasures I first left behind.

For these are my mountains, and this is my glen,
The days of my childhood I'll see them again,
No land ever claimed me though far did I roam,
For these are my mountains and I'm going home.

Figure 56 Raftery Room, Kiltimagh.

In Dublin's Fair City.

In Dublin's fair city, where the girls are so pretty,
I first set my eyes on sweet Molly Malone,
As she wheeled her wheelbarrow,
Through streets broad and narrow,
Crying Cockles and Mussels
Alive, Alive O. Alive, Alive O-o, Alive, Alive O-o,
Crying Cockles and Mussels, Alive, Alive O-o.

Let there be peace.

Let there be peace for today and forever,
May troubles cease for this fair land we love,
With hope and prayer that our fears will be ended,
When God hears our prayer let there be peace.

Peace to tend the fields of grain,
Watch the sky or sea,
Walk in sunshine or in rain,
Unafraid and free,
Peace in our time,
And for our children's children,
God of our fathers hear us,
Let there be peace.

Daisy, daisy, give me your answer do.

Daisy, daisy, give me your answer do.
I'm half-crazy all for the love of you,
It won't be a stylish marriage,
I can't afford a carriage,
But you'll look neat, upon the seat,
Of a bicycle made for two.

Moonlight in Mayo.

When Irish eyes are smiling sure it's like a morn in spring,
When Irish hearts are happy,
All the world seems bright and gay,
And when Irish eyes are smiling,
Sure, they'd steal your heart away.

Roll out the barrel.
Roll out the barrel,
We'll have a barrel of fun,
Roll out the barrel,
We've got the blues on the run,
Zing! Boom! Tarrarel,
Now's the time to roll out the barrel,
For the gang's all here,

My Bonnie lies over the ocean.

My Bonnie lies over the ocean,
My Bonnie lies over the sea,
My Bonnie lies over the ocean,
Oh! Bring back My Bonnie to me.

Just a song at twilight.

Just a song at twilight,
When the lights are low,
And the flickering shadows,
Softly come and go.

Though the heart be weary,
Sad the day and long,
Still to us at twilight,
Comes Love's old song,
Comes Love's old sweet song.

Galway Bay.

If you ever go across the sea to Ireland,
It may be at the closing of your day,
Just to see again the moon rise over Claddagh,
And watch the sun go down on Galway Bay.

To see again the ripple on a trout stream,
And the women in the meadows making hay,
Just to sit beside a log fire in a cabin,
And watch the barefoot gossoons at their play.

And if there is going to be a life hereafter,
And somehow, I feel sure there is going to be,
I will ask my God to let me make my Heaven,
In that dear land across the Irish sea.

Show me the way to go home.

Show me the way to go home,
I'm tired and I want to go to bed,
I had a little drink about an hour ago,
And it's gone right to my head.

Wherever I may roam, on Land or Sea or Foam,
You can always hear me singing this song,
Show me the way to go home.

When Irish hearts are happy,
all the world seems bright and gay,
And when Irish eyes are smiling,
Sure, they'd steal your heart away.

Roll out the barrel, we'll have a barrel of fun,
Roll out the barrel, we've got the blues on the run,
Zing! Boom! Tarrarel, Now's the time to roll out the barrel,
For the gang's all here,

My Bonnie lies over the ocean,
My Bonnie lies over the sea,
My Bonnie lies over the ocean,
Oh! Bring back My Bonnie to me.

Just a song at twilight, When the lights are low,
And the flickering shadows, softly come and go,
Though the heart be weary, Sad the day and long,
Still to us at twilight, Come's long old song,
Come's love sweet old song.

If you ever go across the sea to Ireland,
It may be at the closing of your day,
Just to see again the moon rise over Claddagh,
And watch the sun go down on Galway Bay,
To see again the ripple on a trout stream.
And the women in the meadows making hay,
Just to sit beside a log fire in a cabin,
And watch the barefoot gossoons at their play.

And if there is going to be a life hereafter,
And somehow, I feel sure there is going to be,
I will ask my God to make my Heaven,
In that dear land across the Irish sea.

Show me the way to go home,
I'm tired and I want to go to bed,
I had a little drink about a hour ago,
And it's gone right to my head.

Wherever I may roam, on Land or Sea or foam,
You can always hear me singing this song,
Show me the way to go home.

KILTIMAGH PARISH TOWNLANDS AND VILLAGES ~ JOE ROUGHNEEN NT

Annagh Hill	Marshy woods	Anach Choill
Attavalley	Site of town of village	Áit a Bhaile
Ballinamore	Mouth of the big ford	Béal an Attah
Ballinvully	Village on the summit	Baile an Mhullaigh
Ballure	Town (land) of the Yew Tree	Baile Iúr
Bushfield	The hill of the bushes	Croch na Sceagh
Canbrack	Speckled head	Ceann Breac
Carrownteeaun	District with the fairy mount	Ceathrú an tSiain
Carrick	The rock	Carraig
Carrandine	The area of the 4th quarter	Ceathrú an daingin
Cortoon	The quarte	Cearthrun
Cleragh	A stony place	Clochrai
Cloondoolagh	Meadow of the black lake	Cluain dubh loch
Cloonkedagh	Hill field	Cluain Ceadach
Comderry	Crooked oak-grove	Cam dhoire
Corahoor	Marsh of the yew trees	Curragh Iúr
Cordarragh	Hill with oak tree	Corr darrach
Craggagh	Rocky place	Creaga
Cultrasna	Criss-crossing wood	Coill treasna
Cuillalea	Wood of the calf	Coill a' laoigh
Derrykinlough	Oak grove at end of lough	Doire Chinn-locha
Derrybeg	Little oak wood	Doire beag
Derrylahan	Wide oak grove	Doire leathan

Figure 57 Raftery Ireland's blind poet 1780-1835

Derryvohey	Oak wood with hut	Doire an bhoithe
Garryroe	Red Field	Garraí Rua
Gortfada	Long field	Gortfada
Gortgarve	Rough field	Gort Garbh
Gowelboy	Yellow fork (River	Gabhail Bhuí
Greyfield	District of the sheep	Ceathrú na gCaorach
Carrowreagh	Speckled district	Ceathrú Riabhach
Killedan	Lydon's church	Cill Liadain
Larigan	Little Hill	Leargain
Linbawn	White pool	Linn Bán
Lisduff	Black fort	Lios Dubh
Pollagh	Area full of holes	Pollach
Pulronaghnane		Pol Shronachan
Treenagleragh	District of the Clergy	Trian na gCléireach
Treenkeel	Narrow third division	Trian Chaoil
Treenlaur	Narrow third division	Trian Lár
Woods		Coillte

Figure 58 Joe and Molly Roughneen 30 June 1980 Kiltimagh
Photo courtesy of Frank Dolan

HAPPY BIRTHDAY
MIDWEST RADIO

Written by Jerry Walsh

Through lonely hills and valleys,
From the midlands to the sea,
Flows the voice of great Paul Claffey,
The boy from Castlerea.

He started Mid-West Radio,
Ten long years ago,
From the summit of Slieve Cairn,
He made Radio signals go.

To the young and old in Connaught,
He set their hearts aglow,
The Claffey name brought mid-west fame,
From Ballyhaunis in Mayo.

With Jigs and Reels and Ballads grand,
And MIDWEST on parade,
With Irish peat on the beat,
New York history was made.

The nightly prayer with God we share,
Our thoughts so true and warm,
Brave MIDWEST stood the test,
On that December storm.

I have a dream, a lovely dream,
That sometime soon we'll see,
A vison bold - with Paul controlled,
Our own Midwest T.V.

Figure 59 Jerry Walsh with Michael Commins on Midwest Radio telling the Gene Tunney Story c.1999

Figure 60 Midwest Radio in the early 1990's photo courtesy of James Laffey. Midwest Magic and Madness

Staff of Midwest Radio in the early 1990's
L to R: Gerry Glennon,
Maria Mullarkey, Padraic Walsh, Paul Claffey (C.E.O.), Tommy Marren,
Paula Donnellan, Chris Carroll. Photo from Magic and Madness. The
Midwest Phenomenon by James Laffey.

GENE TUNNEY

Gene Tunney: The Fighting Marine and undefeated Heavyweight Boxing Champion of the World.
Dedicated to Mrs Gene Tunney.   Stamford, Connecticut, United States.
Broadcast in serial form on Mid-West   radio, researched, compiled, and presented by Jerry Walsh, Raftery Room, Corner House, Main Street, Kiltimagh, County Mayo, Ireland.
Faithfully aided by Alan Skelton
Recorded by David McGreevy, Main Street, Kiltimagh, helped by Mrs Cora Flynn nee Welsh Great grandniece of Gene Tunney.
Prepared by Paddy Walsh

The Paternal and Maternal Grandparents of Gene Tunney were born in Kiltimagh.

Figure 61 Gene Tunney 1897-1978

Born James Joseph Gene Tunney 25 May 1897 – 7 Nov 1978 was an American professional boxer who competed from 1915 to 1928. He held the world heavyweight title from 1926 to 1928 and retired undefeated in 1928. He held the American light-heavy weight title twice between 1922 and 1923. Total fights: 85. Losses: 1. Wins by K O: 48. Height: 6ft.

Achievements:

1. 23 Sept 1926 Gene Tunney won World Heavyweight Championship beat Jack Dempsey at Sesquicentennial (150 years) Stadium, Philadelphia, Pennsylvania, USA.

2. 22 Sept 1927 Gene Tunney retained the World Heavyweight Championship beat Jack Dempsey at Soldier's Field, Chicago, Illinois, USA (The Long Count)

3. 26 July 1928 at the Yankee Stadium, New York City, New York, USA retained the World Heavyweight Championship beat Tom Heeney.

Tunney spent the winter of 1921 in Northern Ontario, Canada working as a lumberjack to condition himself for his boxing career. If Tunney had imagined that the heavyweight title would bring public acceptance, he was quickly surprised. Weeks after the first Dempsey fight, when the old and new champion presented in the ring at Madison Square Garden, whilst Dempsey got the cheer of the crowd, Tunney's reception consisted of boos and catcalls. Even Dempsey found it embarrassing. Gene Tunney recalled the moment, "Practically overnight, I had become the most unpopular of all the heavyweight champions."

Although Tunney a marine veteran engaged in 85 professional bouts over a 13-year career, barely interrupted by his wartime service (he had nine fights in France in 1918-19, before and after the armistice), his reign as heavyweight champion was brief. He successfully defended in the 1927 Chicago rematch with Dempsey the fabled 'Long Count' fight, in which Tunney was knocked down for the only time in his career, fought brilliantly in stopping the overmatched New Zealander Tom Heeney at Yankee Stadium in 1928, and then a few days later shocked the world by announcing his retirement at the top of his game.

Programme One

Join me now in a walk down memory lane in the footsteps of the famous, with a story of Gene Tunney, undefeated heavyweight champion of the world. I would like to start with his only defeat. Gene Tunney's only defeat in 76 professional fights was in the early 1920's by Harry Grebb, who had the distinction of being the dirtiest fighter in history, light heavy 5ft 8 and half inches, weighing only 11.5 stone, he was famous for his fouls, he was called the 'Pittsburgh Windmill', low, butting, holding and hitting, rubbing his gloves or laces against an opponent's eyes, he had a fierce boxing style, flaying arms in all directions, hence the Windmill name.

He had been middle-weight champion for 3 years. After the fight Gene spent a week in bed. He lost two quarts of blood in the ring, the referee, the floor and Tunney were covered in blood. Harry Grebb gave Tunney a terrible whipping, he broke his nose with a butt, cut his ears and eyes with the laces, his jaw was swollen up to the right temple down along the cheek and up the other side. In those days fights were not stopped, if it were, Gene Tunney would not have beaten Jack Dempsey. During the fight he discovered the way to get inside the Windmill, and he said through clenched teeth he would beat him the next time he met him.

He in fact, beat him three times after that. Grebb died in a car accident some-time later and when he was laid out, it was discovered that he only had sight in one eye, the other eye had no vision for years before. Grebb made a fortune on backing Tunney against Dempsey. Tunney was Chief Pall Bearer at Grebb's funeral

On a day in September in 1926, the news swept through Newtownbrowne Boys National School that Tunney, a Kiltimagh man was the best boxer in the World. As the pupils poured out of the school, every second pair were boxing, jumping, shadowboxing and shouting "Up Tunney" and "Up Kiltimagh". The very busy railway station of the town became alive with excitement. This news arrived in Kiltimagh 65 years ago when Tunney beat Dempsey. I know because I was there, as one of the smaller ones. And, as far as I can remember, I received and gave a few belts or wallops myself on the way home.

**Figure 62 Gene Tunney
USA circa 1925**

Ever since that day, the name Gene Tunney attracted me in a very special way. He was my boyhood hero, and he was a great and wonderful man. As the years went by, I had the pleasure of meeting his three sons John, J.R. and Gene Junior, and I received correspondence from J.R. and his widow Mrs Gene who is a very gracious lady. She is keeping well and lives in Stamford, Connecticut, United States. (Polly Mary Josephine Rowland Lauder Tunney 1907-2008).

Mrs Gene Tunney (Gene's nephew Gene Coughlan and his niece Mary Coughlan, with her husband Dick called recently to the Raftery Room. Mary kindly sent on a package of material and cuttings and items of interest about her uncle Gene, concerning the earlier part of his life and for which I thank her very much.

Almost immediately after the 1926 fight, boxing clubs started up like wildfire all over the country and especially in County Mayo. Each town and village had its club. Remember, at that time we had no cinemas, dance halls, radios or ESB and not many phones or cars. Boxing filled a gap for the younger generation, all trying to follow in the footsteps of the famous Gene Tunney.

Programme Two

With a walk through the village of Cill Aodain we find the old ruins, still called the Tunney homestead. Grandfather John Tunney after being evicted from here moved to Cultrasna (Coill Trasna), and afterwards to a cottage in Aiden Street, where the O'Hara home now stands. Grandfather John died in 1866. All three sons Brian, John and Michael, his three daughters Mary, Ann and Winifred went to America. His widow Bridget Tunney nee Gill remarried Patrick McNicholas from Goulboy, Kiltimagh and died in 1886. There are no known relatives on the Tunney side in the Kiltimagh area as far as I know.

To America at that time also went Mary Lydon of Gortgarve just south of Kiltimagh. This was the maternal home and is still occupied by the Welsh Family on the Lydon side. Mary had three sisters married around Kiltimagh, all fine tall hardy women: Mrs Nicholas Walsh aka Breezy, the old homestead: Mrs Pat Gallagher, Aiden Street and Mrs Mike McDonagh, Cortoonbawn. Cuillalea, Ballinamore, Kiltimagh,

Mary's uncle was Tom Lydon, Kilkelly. Shortly after Mary's arrival in New York, she met and married John Tunney and became the mother of seven. Gene Tunney was christened James Joseph, but his younger brother could not pronounce it and always called him Jane, so the name Gene was finally settled on. They had four daughters Margie, Rose, Maud, and Agnes and three sons John, Gene, and Tom. At ten years old his father presented him with a pair of boxing gloves owing to Genes interest in the sporting columns, especially those of Bob Edgram in the 'New York Evening World'. Edgram's drawings and cartoons excited Gene. On the first day he got the gloves he boxed more rounds than any of the Dempsey bouts, and that was on his tenth birthday. He never forgot the terrible headache he had that night.

**Figure 63 Marty Burke. Jack Dempsey. Gene Tunney. 13 Feb 1924
USA**

The next day, all the neighbouring boys including Gene, had swollen noses and lips, proud badges of honour. At this time, studying Edgram's articles and cartoons of the fights, Gene began to develop the difference between a straight left and a right swing. He took in footballing, broad jumping, the 220-yard dash, and swimming in the river Hudson, and dived from barges, liners, and other high spots. He dived from the upper deck of the S.S. Majestic, and from this height, hands by his side, a soldier's dive, when he hit the water, he received concussion, and had a bad headache for a few days.

Gene Tunney was a street fighter but not a bully. He never missed up the opportunity to fight. This was the training youngsters got in those days, guns were never thought of. Some of the fights would last for three days and would continue after school at different venues. An Irish bricklayer stopped one fight, but most fights were stopped by the neighbourhood police officers. As he got older, he spent more time in the athletic field, the nuns and the parents disliked the street fights and boxing became part of his school activities.

He had one boxing idol. Jack Goodman, who lived on the street in Greenwich Village. As he had no marks on his face from his boxing profession he was referred to as Handsome Jack. Gene used to follow him around as he was a man who was admired by him. He had met all the top notches of his class and was the idol of the West Side.

At the age of 15, Gene decided to go out and conquer the industrial world, his first job was the Ocean Steamship Company. He was an office boy at 5$ a week. After the year he was promoted to mailing clerk and received $11 per week. He soon realised that without further qualifications he could not go far in promotion and joined a correspondence course in mathematics and algebra.

Gene said that algebra and plain geography were not of much assistance in the office or in his life, with one exception, the axion, the shortest distance between two points was a straight line. He used this axion most beneficially in boxing and insisted on applying this principle throughout his boxing career.

Programme Three

About this time at 16 years of age, he met a boy from Greenwich Village, Willie Ward, who had started boxing as a career. He had won several bouts, usually by the knockout route. Gene realised he had beaten this boy earlier, on the streets and backyards. Gene became one of his sparring partners and helped him with his bouts. They moved to larger training quarters and became members of the Greenwich Village Athletic Club.
Gene became acquainted with Willie Greene who was ten years older. He was 26 and had a long boxing career from 17 to 22 years. He fought 168 ring battles, amongst them the toughest lightweights of the period. Gene boxed with Greene for about two years, and learned the art: how to slip, knockdown leads, counter with lefts or rights, sidestep, and avoid being hit unnecessarily, but most important of all, to conserve his energy and time his attacks.

In the beginning the villagers used to say, "let's go down and see Greene make a punchbag of Tunney" but word got round, and soon the big boys were saying "let's go down and see Willie Greene box Tunney". Gene said that the earlier boxing with this dangerous fellow made a careful boxer of him, and this cautiousness always remained part of his boxing technique.

Around this period, he became very interested in skills and carefully watched from the ringside and developed his own ideas of technique and effective points, so much so that Willie Greene eventually realised that Gene Tunney was more than a match and refused to put on the gloves with him. However, he had pride and respect for Gene and wanted to exhibit him. This respect was mutual.

At this stage, Gene was accepted as the best boxer in Greenwich Village, which brought him to the attention of Billy Jacobs, who was the 'matchmaker' of the Sharkey Athletic Club. Jacobs wanted Gene to turn professional but Gene at this time had two jobs. He was still with the Steamship Company, and he also was an instructor in athletics and club organiser on the board of education public school 41.

Jacobs talked to Gene and a man called Eddie O'Brien, a saloonkeeper who was watching Gene's boxing bouts with great interest. Eddie knew a great deal about prize fighting and belonged to the Avonia Athletic Club which had turned out great fighters including Jack Goodman, Harry Schumaker, Tommy Maloney, Kid Black including Jimmy who later became Mayor of New York. Even so, Eddie was confident that Tunney was the greatest fighter he had ever seen. They all finally induced Gene to accept a match with a tough fighter called Bobby Dawson. It was the custom of boxers to weigh-in, in the presence of each other. Dawson got on the scale and wanted to know where Tunney was. Being told that Tunney was still in the dressing room and that this was his first professional fight, he barged into Tunney's dressing room shouting, "Where is Tunney?" "Where is Tunney?" Tunney sitting in a corner with his trunks and shoes on said quickly "I am here". Dawson growled "I want to see you on the scales". Tunney asked "Where are they? and was told they were outside.

When Tunney stood up to follow Dawson, Dawson turned around, looked at Tunney, taking in his long slim arms, thin waist, and long neck, and

Figure 64 Gene Tunney 'A man must fight'.

sneeringly remarked "Go over and sit down, I don't care if you weigh a ton". Gene sat down quietly and thought this Dawson is an experienced fighter. Looking at me, he will come to the conclusion I am not a fighter. This added to Tunney's timidness and subdued mood, resulting in Dawson's confidence growing, and that he would dash from his corner in the first round and try to bully his opponent.

This is exactly what happened, but after running into six or seven straight lefts, Dawson timed his rushes more carefully. Gene felt the strain during the fifth round, his arms got heavy, and his legs began to tremble. During the seventh round, Dawson was coming in with a wild upper cut, Gene, completely weary succeeded in catching him and knocked him down. The count reached nine when the bell rang, and Dawson did not come up for the eighth round. This was Tunney's first professional fight and for this pugilistic effort he was paid $18. He gave $6 to Greene, Eddie O'Brien refused to accept his $6 and never accepted a dollar from Gene for his workouts. To celebrate the occasion, Gene gave a dinner to the rest of the boys at Rockaway Beach.

Programme Four

We'll hear today about the Long Count, which is still talked about around the world. **"A Man Must Fight"** by Gene Tunney - "*When my story is told, I'll tell it myself, and I'll write it myself. It may not be great literature, but it will be the truth*".

Thus, spoke Gene Tunney, (conqueror of the terrible Dempsey) after four years of hounding by editors who besought him for his story of his rise to the winning and defending of the Heavyweight Championship of the World. But here Ladies and gentlemen, here it is, all of it. Here are the punches and politics of prize fighting and written by the man who did the fighting.
Listen, there's a bell.

Tunney leads: "Jack Dempsey and I have fought 20 rounds. I have whipped him in 19 of them. That seems to settle for all time the question as to who (the better man is) is the better man. I want to give credit to Dempsey for his gameness, his fighting ability and his punching power. I do not want to take away from him one iota of credit for that seventh round in Chicago, the round in which he knocked me down. I got a little careless and I paid the penalty with a trip to the canvas, but it was all foolishness to say that I was in real danger of being counted out. I made up my mind to take the count of nine. That was one of the first things I was taught in boxing, to take the count of nine in the event of a knockdown.

Until that Chicago fight, I never have been forced to bring that bit of knowledge into play. All the time that I was down, I was in full possession of my faculties. I knew what was going on and followed the count carefully. Here I want to say Referee Harry Barry warned us that no count would be started if the scorer did not move into the neutral corner. Dempsey has been in the ring long enough to be calm and cool under circumstances such as those which attended the scoring of the knockdown. He should have known enough to move at once into a neutral corner. Instead, he remained in his own corner, too excited to remember his instruction and one of the cardinal rules of the ring.

It has been charged by some critics, that if the knockdown had been scored in the middle of the ring, instead of out at the ropes where I had a chance to pull myself up, I would have been counted out. There is nothing to this assertion. Had we been in the middle of the ring, I would not have been knocked down. The ropes prevented me from moving out of danger. While on the subject of the knockdown, I want to give my own impressions of this exciting event. The motion pictures show that I got six punches leading to the knockdown. I remember only three of them, the last of which hit me as I was going down. My first feeling on hitting the canvas was one of relief. It felt good to be on the ground out of danger. It felt good to be out of the range of any more punches and at the same time in possession of my faculties.

Figure 65 Gene Tunney's Jacket a gift from the Tunney
family to Jerry and Paddy Walsh.

Safe in the knowledge that I could get up on the count of nine I did just that and then I retreated. It has been said that I ran away. I never have run away from any man, in or out of the ring and I did not have to run away from Jack Dempsey that night. But I did retreat from his fire. I knew he was dangerous at that particular minute and that the longer I could hold him off the better equipped I would be to go through with my plan to launch a terrific counterattack. I knew I had Dempsey when he stopped and motioned sneeringly for me to come out and fight. It was the gesture of a baffled fighter.

I refused to heed his sneers or pay attention to the howls of the crowd. It was my championship, my title to defend, my reputation to guard. I knew that to rush in and fight at that time might have been fatal. I flatter myself that I kept my head and fought back my instinct to accept Dempsey's challenge and exchange blows with him. I bided my time, cleared my head, and then went to it, and the results in the eighth, ninth and tenth rounds more than vindicated my judgement and decision to rest for a while before going after the challenger.

All throughout my ring career I had planned against the time when I would be knocked down. I had made up my mind to do one of two things, jump up at once on a counterattack to hide my condition or take a series of counts to clear my head. I had planned to go down again for nine from another punch and go down for a third time if necessary. But all those plans went into the disregard and proved as well that it is futile to make up your mind ahead of time about things to be done in extreme emergencies. I made a new plan the moment I was floored, I took my nine, waited to clear my head just as any sane fighter would have done and then battered Dempsey around the ring.

Dempsey still persists that he is the better man. The story of the fight, the pictures, Dempsey's own impressions all shout to the contrary. Dempsey had two chances against me, and he failed twice. I will be ready, but it seems to me that Dempsey has run out of rope.

I will be ready in a year to defend the title again. I believe that next September will be the right time, as that is the best time of the year for a heavyweight Championship. In the meantime, I will keep fit, no matter what I decide to do in the interim, do a motion picture or anything else, the boxing followers of this country may rest assured that Gene Tunney will not soften up from easy living.

And now **"The Long Count"** by Harry Barry

Little did I realise when I was called into the office by the Illinois State Boxing Commission to receive the assignment to referee the Tunney/Dempsey battle that I would become the subject of worldwide controversy. The honour of being selected for this most important post in such gigantic sports affair, naturally made me joyous. I then and there resolved that I would treat both fighters with the utmost equality and that I would enforce the rules of the Illinois Board to the best of my ability.

I have been accused by Jack Dempsey of being partial, but I feel confident that the public, the boxing officials, and the seconds of Dempsey know in their hearts, that I did what was expected of me. I went into that ring in Soldier's Field and one thing was uppermost in my mind, the fact that on the honesty of that contest, on the actions of fighters, judges and referee, rested the future of boxing. Before the fight we were instructed to follow the rules to the letter. We were told what was expected of us, and in turn told the fighters just what was expected of them for they were part of the contract.

The Two Seconds knew what would be expected of their men, for they spent many hours in the offices of the boxing commission going over every minute detail. Yet, following the bout I am accused by Dempsey's handlers of showing favouritism and preventing a knocked-out fighter to continue and then carry off the honours.

Figure 66 1926 USA Gene Tunney Stamp

What a ridiculous stand for Leo P. Moran to take! How foolish of him to urge Dempsey, a fine sportsman, to sign his name to such a statement when Jack Dempsey was to blame for the entire muddle, if such it be called! When Dempsey and Tunney joined me in the ring, I asked Gene who his Chief Second was "Jimmy Bunsen" he replied. Dempsey, in answer to a similar question, said Leo Flynn".

I then instructed the Chief Seconds as follows: "You are the only men whom I recognise in the corners, and I will expect you to maintain order and so forth in your respective corners".

Then I turned to Tunney and Dempsey, and I said: "You fellows are boxing straight Queensberry rules, hands are free and when you are locked, I will tell you to break and each of you must immediately take a half step backward. This break must be clean, I won't tolerate any sneak punches.

In the case of a knock-down, the man on his feet will immediately retire to the farthest neutral corner and will remain there until the fallen man is on his feet or until he has been counted out. "Do you understand?" Both answered in the affirmative. I then asked, if there was anything else either wanted to take up, and each said no, there was not. I told them shake hands and come out fighting. It is a pleasure to say that both boys obeyed my commands implicitly and I had no trouble with them until the seventh round.

The knock-down occurred about four or five feet from Dempsey's corner and tight against the ropes on the west side of the ring as Tunney hit the floor his eyes had a glassy expression, and it was apparent he was quite badly hurt. Dempsey, possibly through force of habit, or perhaps through forgetfulness failed to go to a neutral corner which would have brought him immediately behind Tunney. The time-keeper's count had started but seeing his action I thrust my arm in front of him and ordered Jack to a neutral corner.

Figure 67 Senator John Tunney. Micheál Higgins. Michael Charlton. Senator Ted Kennedy. Susan Carroll. Jerry Walsh. John Carroll.

Dempsey persisted however and tried to circle round me, in the other direction, then apparently realising he really was punishing himself, he turned and walked quickly to the south-east corner.

Then. I immediately turned to face the timekeeper and by holding up my index finger signalled him "one" took up the count and I fell in with his cadence and counted up to Nine when Tunney arose, and the contest was resumed.

My impression of Tunney after he had been knocked down, was that he regained his senses within three or four seconds and even though Dempsey had immediately retired to the neutral corner as per instructions. He, Tunney would have been able to jump up in good shape before the final count. I think it was a great fight and there is no doubt who won it.

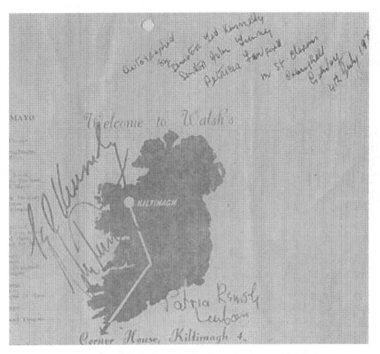

Figure 68 Kennedy, Tunney, Lawford, 4 July 1974 Galway, Ireland

Programme Five

We now hear about the Long Count as described by that leading sportswriter, Nat Fleisher in November 1927. Fleischer was boxing correspondent for the 'Ring Boxing Magazine'. He was in the ringside for The Third Battle of the Century. The Third Battle of the Century has passed into ring history and with it, the realisation that Gene Tunney, is the successful defender of his World Heavyweight Championship. Nat Fleisher confirmed the fighting game now has a worthy successor to the greatest crown wearers of the past.

Gene, 'The Fighting Marine', who was mocked coast to coast by those who never gave him credit for being a real champion. He met every test and came through with flying colours. True, the strong Dempsey adherents continued to shout from the house tops that the "Manassa Mauler" was deprived of a knockout through poor judgement of the referee, but their arguments cannot pass the acid test. Gene Tunney won the Chicago battle fairly, and in so doing he demonstrated that he is Dempsey's master. Dempsey and Tunney might yet engage in a third meeting, but if they do, the result will be the same, but damaging for Dempsey. In that thrilling bout at Soldier's Field, Chicago, Gene out-boxed his Coast rival in seven of the ten rounds, took Dempsey's hardest blows, came back with a whirlwind finish after being on the verge of a knock-out and in the last three rounds outboxed Dempsey to the extent that the Manassa Mauler could scarcely finish the final session.

Does this show championship calibre on the part of the conqueror? We'll say it does! It takes quick thinking, nimble wits, and strong agile legs to go through what Tunney termed was Hell for him in that memorable seventh round and survive the session. Those are the assets of a real champion.
Did Tunney falter, as would less hardy, brainless fighters when that terrible left hook of Dempsey's crossed against his chin after five other blows were landed? Not the Fighting Marine! He had been on the battlefield of France and the word 'QUIT' was not found in his language. Yet, sitting there in the third row of the working press, seats in Chicago, gazing intensely on the fallen form of New York's own, I heard many of the Western newspaper men yell at Gene: "Get up, you quitter". And a few minutes later, when those same fellas each one a strong Dempsey adherent, saw Gene on his feet again and circling the ring for more than a minute and a half to avoid the deadly wallop of the former champion, again a cry went up: "You yellow dog, fight, why won't you?"

What an unsportsmanlike indictment against as game a fellow as ever graced the ring! Would these men and thousands of others in that gigantic gathering, have given Tunney credit for the game, had he stood in the centre of the ring a target for Jack's finishing punches? No, Gentlemen let's be reasonable and unbiased, Gene Tunney had two choices in that seventh round. When he arose, he could either have elected to fight it out with his then stronger opponent, or to keep out of Jack's way by circling him for the rest of the session.

Had Gene selected the former, he would undoubtedly have been knocked-out and a ring history would have been made in the first crowning of a heavyweight champion who previously had lost his title. Gene chose correctly, a splendid test of a champion brainwashing, and for this, he was termed 'yellow'. Compare his quick-wittedness with the slow thinking of Dempsey. Jack had two choices in that round, just as did Gene. He could have elected to hasten to a neutral corner, as agreed by the principles before the battle in the commission office and in the ring, or to station himself over his fallen prey as he did in the Firpo fight.
Unfortunately, Dempsey chose wrongly and with that choice lost whatever chance he had to regain the world's heavyweight title. Again, when the fight was resumed, Dempsey had another opportunity to win the contest, but again made the wrong choice. The Dempsey who fought Jess Willard or the Dempsey who knocked out Louis Firpo, would never have deliberated as did Jack after Tunney arose and started to safety. That Dempsey with the killer instinct would have leaped at Gene helter-skelter, cornered him, and knocked him out before the round could be completed. Instead, he decided to follow Gene around the ring.

The youthful agile Tunney, the finest specimen of physical manhood in our midst – this is the fellow the ageing Jack Dempsey, with his weary legs and fatigued body, tried to follow. Gene's thinking powers told him Dempsey found the handicap too great and in disgust he suddenly stopped short and yelled at the champion: "Quit your running. Come on, fight". Here again Tunney proved to be Dempsey's superior with his quick thinking and tactical manoeuvres. These are great assets, and in these, Gene proved the master.

He was the champion, every inch of him, Should Tunney be condemned for protecting himself through perfect brainwork? Gene, the receiver of the rights and lefts which brought him down, in that trying seventh round. Those six terrible punches, and he came through the crisis with a far higher rating than did the man who scored the knockdown. That's where the champion quality comes in. Tunney has it and let us make no mistake about that moment. Tunney was there in the pinch and that enabled him to retain the title. Let us sing his praises. He certainly deserves commendation. The last three rounds of the battle demonstrated fully the ability of the champion. Gene, just back from what looked like a certain knockout, uncorked that left of his and realising the urgency of keeping Dempsey away from him, he pecked and pecked almost at will with that portside paw, then suddenly shot out his right. A right chop brought Dempsey down, the blow coming after the left had placed Jack off balance. Although Dempsey took no count, the knockdown convinced the spectators that Tunney had not been hurt much when he was floored. Analysing the bout from a spectator's point of view, I feel that there can be absolutely no reason for questioning the decision, even on the basis of a long count.

Gene Tunney was Jack's superior in everything but the punch, and even in this, Gene excelled by a slight margin. Gene is not the knockout or hitter that Dempsey was in his prime, but Dempsey remarked after the fight: "If you fellows think Tunney can't hit, you have another guess coming. Say he can hit as hard as any fellow in the boxing game".

In the matter of punches, Gene landed almost twice as many as did Dempsey. As a matter of fact, in the eighth ninth and tenth round, he scored a little over three to one for Gene on blows landed on Dempsey and many were of a stinging variety. In these rounds Dempsey could not even land the forbidden rabbit punch which he used throughout the fight. True he mixed these with the ordinary, but the bulk of the blows sent to Gene's neck were the rabbit punches without as much as a whisper coming from the champion. That showed Gene in his true colours. A champion who was in the ring to win not at any cost but by fair ring tactics, he did not want to retain the title by being declared the winner of a foul.

So much for the analysis of the fight. Now for the count which offered such widespread discussion and will continue to be the subject of controversy for many months. That Gene Tunney received a long count goes without question. That the count was justified by the failure of Dempsey to go to a neutral corner, also goes without question. The Illinois Boxing Commission's rules state that when a boxer is floored the referee shall begin the count over him and if he does not arise at ten, he shall be counted out.

Under the rules, the referee need not count until the fighter who is on his feet reaches a neutral corner. The referee does not have to pick up the timekeeper's count. Unfortunately for Dempsey, the rule proved disastrous, but had he adhered to the letter of his agreement he never would have found himself in such a predicament.

Law is law and rules are rules and they must be obeyed. Dempsey and Tunney had agreed to them, and therefore no matter how ill the wind fared, Referee Barry followed the rules as laid down to all hands, he was justified in his ring actions. There are some, those who bet on Dempsey, who openly declared Jack was robbed and that the bout was framed for Gene to win. Most ridiculous, say we. There are others who insist that Tunney never would have been able to rise to his feet had the count been proper. Conjecture, we say.

It is questionable and subject to discussion. True, Gene appeared rather weak and glassy eyed for at least four of the thirteen seconds he was down, but it must be remembered that he kept looking at the proceedings, watching the referee chase Dempsey to a neutral corner, and then took his full allotment of time before rising. Therefore, it seems only plausible that Gene would have gotten up before the count of ten, had been required. He was not groggy.

The mere fact that Gene was able within two seconds after the count to dance around the ring while on his toes, proves perfectly that he was not in any danger after the first few seconds. The further fact that the hardest blow he landed on Dempsey came towards the end of that same round, a terrific right to the stomach that almost doubled Jack, also bears out this contention. Furthermore, it was this blow that practically settled Jack's chances for winning the crown. He lost heart then and there.

Jack Dempsey came out in the eighth round with a haggard look, shuffling feet and generally seemed downcast, both as a result of feeling he was deprived of a knockout which he felt he had justly gained, and because of Gene's quick comeback. The championship calibre of Tunney was brought forth conclusively in that eighth round and the subsequent two rounds.

That right chop to the ear which dropped Dempsey in the eighth, took a little more of the starch out of the former champion. He simply could not understand how a fighter floored by him, and almost out in the previous session, could punish him so much in the following round. Gene Tunney, it must be remembered, is the first fighter to weather the storm after being floored by the Manassa Mauler. Is it any wonder then, that Dempsey seemed befuddled?

Programme Six

The one and only Micheál O'Hehir, loved by everybody, on hearing of Gene Tunney's death, in November 1978, paid a lovely tribute to him in the Sunday Press, the headline read 'The gentleman that was Gene Tunney' and I quote: "The death during the week at the age of 80 of former world heavyweight boxing champion Gene Tunney has meant the departure of yet another great name from the world of international sport".

In the case of Gene Tunney, it is the passing of a man who brought respectability to the much-maligned world of professional boxing, a respect which unfortunately is now a thing of the past. I had the pleasure of meeting this handsome former Marine in the mid 1960's at his stockbrokers office in the Pan Am building in New York.

Figure 69 Micheal O'Hehir

We were brought together by a mutual friend, and it be impossible to describe how co-operative Tunney was with myself and the crew who were there to interview him on T.V. There was an almost austere manner about the one-time marine who came out of the forces to become a professional boxer "until I got enough money to quit the business" as he put it.

Christened James Joseph Tunney he will go down in history as the man who was involved in two tremendous fights with Jack Dempsey, including the historic long count. This was in the Soldier's Field in Chicago a year after he had taken the title from Dempsey. The two men fought two bloody battles, Dempsey's face was like a pulp after the first, and the controversy about the long count would be enough to cause a life-time rift between two lesser men. The fact is that they became good friends down through the years. Gene helped the more flamboyant Dempsey by publicly frequenting the now defunct Jack Dempsey Restaurant on Broadway in the early days and indeed when family trouble struck, either of the men was on hand for each other.

In round 7 of their return bout in 1927, an aggressive Dempsey caught up with the boxing Tunney, who had been elusive, and brought him to the canvas with two left hooks to the jaw followed by a right. Dempsey stood over Tunney as he had done with Firpo, but the local referee, Dave Barry, instead ordered the anxious Jack Dempsey to retire to a corner. Jack eventually went, and only then did the count by the referee start. Nobody gives an exact account of the number of seconds that elapsed, but Gene Tunney recalled that he was on one knee preparing to jump up when the count reached nine. It was delayed so long that his head was totally cleared when nine was counted and he resumed.

His description to me of that round indicates the type of man Tunney was, "In pursuit of my professional occupation, I listened to the referee and ignored Jack Dempsey" "I suppose I was very fortunate, but though he came at me fiercely afterwards, I was sufficiently in the lead at the end to win" While this was the fight which put Gentleman Gene in the history books, he was more affected by his two fights with Harry Grebb. "He was a fierce man. He broke my nose and beat me pitifully in our first fight" Grebb won that – the only professional loss for Tunney, who bravely insisted on a rematch and put the record straight before his Dempsey and world championship encounters.

Dignified in manner, massively so in appearance, Gene Tunney was a recognised student of Shakespeare, on whom he gave lectures in Yale University. He was a friend of professors and the literary including George Bernard Shaw. He married the socialite Polly Lauder of the Carnegie family, and one of their four sons John, was a United States Senator from California. There is no argument Gene Tunney was a credit to his sport. As we move along Memory Lane towards the last Count, I sincerely hope that the young and the future generations enjoy the story of Gentleman Gene Tunney, undefeated heavyweight champion of the world, and as the final bell rings, the truth and action of the rightful winner of the famous Long Count, will still be talked about around the world in the years that are to come.

Written by Jerry Walsh. 1918-2005 Raftery Room, Kiltimagh. Mayo, Ireland

Figure 70 Polly and Gene Tunney

GEORGE BERNARD SHAW GENE TUNNEY "THE POWER OF PRAYER"

This incident happened in September 1929, as direct result George Bernard Shaw wrote to Sister Laurentia, the Abbess of Stanbrook Abbey, Stanbrook Abbey in Wass, North Yorkshire is an abbey originally built as a contemplative house for Benedictine nuns. The community was founded in 1625 in Cambrai, Flanders, then part of the Spanish Netherlands under the auspices of the English Benedictines. His letters were produced in a play "The Best of Friends" in Olney theatre, Maryland, United States starring Pauline Flanagan, County Sligo, Joe Dowling 1996. Shaw and Sister Laurentia were friends for many years George Bernard Shaw (26 July 1856-2 Nov 1950) wrote this letter in 1949.

Figure 71 Polly Lauder Tunney

Dear Sister, Laurentia,

A few weeks ago, I had a visit from another special friend whose vocation was as widely different from yours as any two vocations on earth can be, and yet who is connected in my thoughts with your subject, the efficacy of prayer. He is Gene Tunney, and Irish American, still famous as the Undefeated Heavyweight Champion of the World, no less. He is a good man all through and entirely presentable in any society. He comes from a devout Catholic family, pillars of the Church, but, as he puts, "When I went into the ring as a professional, I dropped all that".

But though he dropped the faith it did not drop him. He made a fortune from his fights and when he retired, he married a rich woman. The young couple came travelling to Europe and found themselves on a pleasure Island in the Adriatic when I met him and made friends with him. He told me what had just happened to him. His young wife was attacked by a very rare complaint, unknown to most surgeons, of a double appendicitis. Nothing but a major operation could save her, and there was on the Island one old and useless doctor. Death within ten hours was certain. Gene, helpless and desperate, could only watch her die. Except one thing, to go back to his faith and pray. He prayed. Next morning very early there landed on the Island the most skilful surgeon in Germany, the discoverer of double appendices. Before ten o'clock Mrs Tunney was out of danger and is now the healthy mother of four children. Protestants and sceptics see nothing in this but a coincidence, but even one coincidence is improbable, and a bundle of them as in this case hardly credible in a world full of miracles. The prayer, the timing of the surgeon's arrival, his specialisation for the rare disease, were so complicatedly coincidental that if they had been reported from China about strangers, I should have not believed the story. As it is, I do not doubt it: and it goes to confirm the value I instinctively set on your prayers. So do not forget me in them.

I cannot explain how or why I am the better for them: but I like them and am certainly not the worse. Perhaps, I have told you the Tunney story before, old men tend to repeat their stories mercifully. No matter, it will bear twice telling. (checks his pocket watch) I am so very old (Ninety-Two) that you would hardly know me if I could now go to Stanbrook. I am very groggy on my legs and make blunders by the dozen, but although my body is going to bits, I have passed the second childhood that comes at eighty or thereabouts and got that clear second wind that follows it. My soul still marches on. Do not for a moment feel bound to answer this, you have no time for duty letters. A hail on my next birthday, if it ever arrives, will satisfy me.

George Bernard Shaw
GB Shaw 1949
Nobel Prize Winner
1925 for Literature

Figure 72 George Bernard Shaw.

BY THE WAY

BY THE WAY --- POETRY COULD EXTEND YOUR LIFE

Aiden Burke from Gortgarve Kiltimagh spoke these thoughtful words. Aiden a retired St. Louis Secondary School teacher and Kiltimagh historian encouraged and pushed Jerry Walsh to produce his book Kiltimagh 4 in 2005 We all have heard of the importance of a balanced diet, plenty of sleep and regular exercise if you want to live a long and healthy life.

But would it not be great if visits to the theatre or art galleries be part of this longevity? Well, it seems this could be the case, with research published in the British Medical Journal revealing that the more people engage with the arts, the lower their risk of an early death.

The effects were substantial. Women and men aged 50 plus who saw a play, attended the opera or went to the museum, gallery or concert every few months were almost a third less likely to die early than those who never engaged with such activities. Even dabbling in the arts once or twice a year cut the risk of dying by 14%.

These results cannot be explained away by virtue of culture vultures being wealthier, rather, it seems the outcome is at least partly due to them being more likely to look for health advice. The outings may also provide exercise, combat loneliness and stimulate the brain.

Another fun and more budget-friendly way to exercise the mind is to learn a piece of poetry. In Broadcaster Gyles Brandreth's book "Dancing by the Light of the Moon", he encouraged us to go back to learning poetry as we did at school.

Most of us will feel that we no longer have the memory to do so, but Brandreth, who took the time to interview neuroscience experts at Cambridge Unitarity, informs us that the issue is not the actual memorising, it is the recall that is needed afterwards, and recall will improve with practice.

Learning a new poem every week, even just a rude limerick, will not only exercise the relevant neurological muscles, it will also lift your heart. What better way to extend your life than reading poetry or even better still compose it!

MEMORIAL CARD
PADDY JOHN JOE AND JERRY

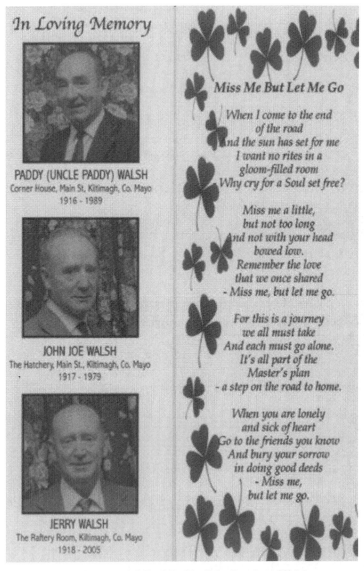

In Loving Memory

PADDY (UNCLE PADDY) WALSH
Corner House, Main St., Kiltimagh, Co. Mayo
1916 - 1989

JOHN JOE WALSH
The Hatchery, Main St., Kiltimagh, Co. Mayo
1917 - 1979

JERRY WALSH
The Raftery Room, Kiltimagh, Co. Mayo
1918 - 2005

Miss Me But Let Me Go

When I come to the end
of the road
And the sun has set for me
I want no rites in a
gloom-filled room
Why cry for a Soul set free?

Miss me a little,
but not too long
And not with your head
bowed low.
Remember the love
that we once shared
- Miss me, but let me go.

For this is a journey
we all must take
And each must go alone.
It's all part of the
Master's plan
- a step on the road to home.

When you are lonely
and sick of heart
Go to the friends you know
And bury your sorrow
in doing good deeds
- Miss me,
but let me go.

Figure 73 Memorial Card Paddy, John Joe, Jerry Walsh.

JERRY'S BROCHURE

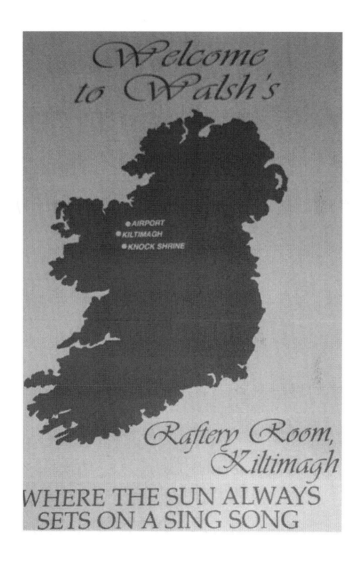

Figure 74 Raftery Room Brochure

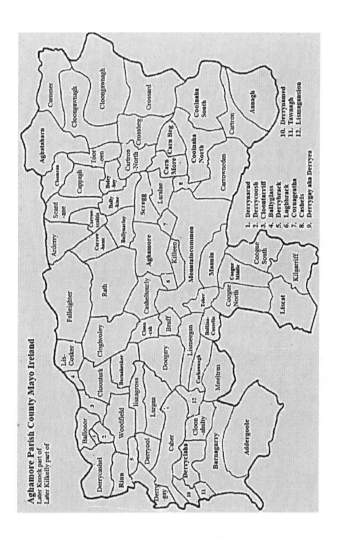

Figure 75 Map of Aghamore Parish. County Mayo, Ireland

Figure 76 Map of Kilcolman Parish Claremorris

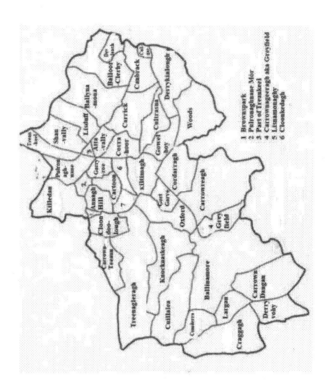

Figure 77 Map of Kiltimagh Killedan Parish Mayo Ireland

Figure 78 Map of Bohola Parish Mayo Ireland

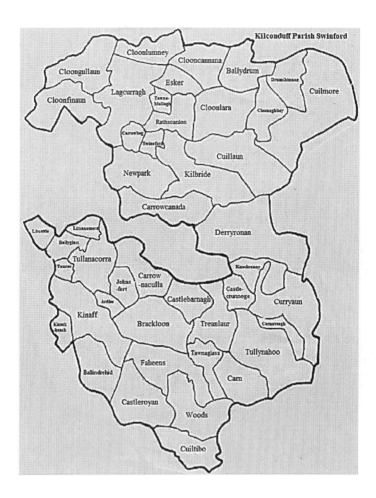

Figure 79 Map of Kilconduff Parish Swinford

Figure 80 Map of Meelick Parish County Mayo Ireland

WALSH FAMILY TREE

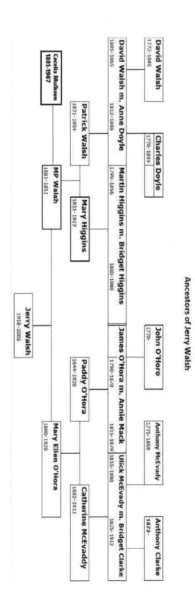

Figure 81 Ancestors of Jerry Walsh, Kiltimagh.

THE WALSH FAMILY OF GAULBOY AKA GOWELBOY IN THE REGISTRY OF DEEDS

There is a Memorial in the Registry of Deeds concerning the lease of lands by George Browne of Brownstown, Co Mayo to David and James Walsh of Gaulboy, Kiltimagh, Co Mayo, Ireland. This memorial occupies most of page 11 of Book 487 numbered 303734. It is dated 25 May 1792.

The Deed of Lease was between George Browne of Brownstown, Co Mayo, and David Walsh and James Walsh. George Browne demised, granted and set 20a 2r 36p located in Kiltimagh to David Walsh and James Walsh, lands which are now held and enjoyed by James and David Walsh. The lease runs for the natural lives of David Walsh, John Walsh, son of James Walsh and the life of John Walsh, son of David Walsh. The above-mentioned parties have to pay a yearly rent of £8.0.0 in two equal payments, every May 1st and November 1st. This rent is over and above all taxes and country charges. The tenants, James and David Walsh and their heirs, bind themselves on the penalty of £15.0.0 that they will reclaim 3 acres of bog before the expiry of the lease. The said tenants are to build two houses, 13-foot-wide 14-foot-long and 9-foot-high with stone lime and mortar within two perches of the road leading from Kiltimagh to Cloonfallagh. Each house must be built before the expiry of the lease, and they should be allowed £5.0.0 for the building of each house. In the case of failure to carry out the building, the parties will forfeit £20.0.0.

Witnesses: Patt Egan, Kiltimagh. Alex McDonald

Signed: David Walsh (seal) Patt Egan swore that he saw David Walsh sign the lease on 12 January 1792.

Comments

The reference in the Registry of Deeds is Book 487, page 11, Deed number 303734.

"Demise, grant and set" are part of a formula used in Deeds of Lease and they all mean the same thing, namely, to lease.

"Lease of lives" this was quite a common type of lease up until the 1840s. No exact period of time was given and, since there was little or no inflation, the value of the rent remained the same. The lease of lives given here is for the lives of David and James Walsh and their sons; we have no idea how old any of these people were; in all probability, John Walsh, son of David Walsh and John Walsh son of James Walsh were youngsters. In theory at least, the lease would be up for negotiation on the death of the last person mentioned in the lease.

The conditions attached to the lease are quite interesting. We can see from them that George Browne of Brownstown (not far from Ballinrobe) was an "improving" landlord. His aim was to have his tenants reclaim land from bog and to build solid stone walled houses for themselves and their families. The Walsh brothers must have had turbary rights on the bog which, by that time, must have been cut away. There was plenty of time given to carry out this reclamation work. I have no idea where the brothers had the bog; all I remember is Jim Walsh (known to us by his nickname as "Jim Davey") having a bog near us in The Woods. The original turbary rights were probably on a different bog. They were very strong and big people—the modern version of the "JCB digger" or to borrow a phrase used in England years ago "Dig down deep, throw far back".

The specifications laid down for the houses are quite interesting. The specifications given for the length and breadth of the house were 13 feet by 14 feet. Clearly, this is a one roomed house, and the construction materials were to be stone, lime and mortar. This is a clear move away from the mud and wattle cabins of earlier times. The height of the walls was standard at the time and the roof was made of thatch presumably.

The intention of the landlord seems to have been to improve the standard of accommodation of his tenants not by building houses for them but by encouraging them to build the houses themselves to his specifications. And this was accompanied by a reward; they were allowed £5.0.0 for the build; this may have been a kind of rebate on the rent.

When the Deed of Lease was signed on May 25th, 1792, the Walsh brothers had already been tenants of George Brown. They were obviously tenants in good standing as they received a lease of lives in that year. This puts the Walsh family in Gaulboy from about the 1750s or even earlier though we have no documentary proof of this.

The memorial of this lease, that is, a short summary of the contents of the lease, was lodged with the Registry of Deeds nearly two years later, on 12ᵗʰ January 1794; it was presumably signed by other tenants of good standing, in particular, by Patt Egan.

Alex Mc Donald (Kilmovee area) is not a name with which I would be familiar from the Tithe Applotment Books, a generation later; although that does not mean that he wasn't in Kiltimagh at that time. Aiden Feerick the Professional Genealogist provided this summary to us.

Thank you to Aiden Feerick Genealogist for your great help in transcribing this Memorandum and for making it understandable. Thank you to Betty Solan and Peter Sobolewski for this reference in your book "Kiltimagh. Our lives and Times". Thank you to Nancy Reeb Genealogy and her husband Fred. The village of Gaulboy is also known as Goulboy and Gowelboy.

LEASE OF LAND 1792 TO DAVID AND JAMES WALSH.

Figure 82 Lease for Land 1792 David Walsh. James Walsh

Figure 83 Raftery Pipe Band

Figure 84 Ruane Fire in Kiltimagh 1944

L to R: Jerry Walsh, Tommie Sweeney worked in Mulhern's John Joe Walsh, John James Kelly PO and Michael J Meenaghan. Ruane house fire. Eight people died in the fire on 18th May 1944 at Main Street, Kiltimagh.

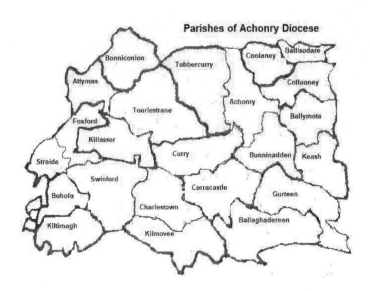

Figure 85 Achonry Diocese

RAFTERY THE BLIND POET

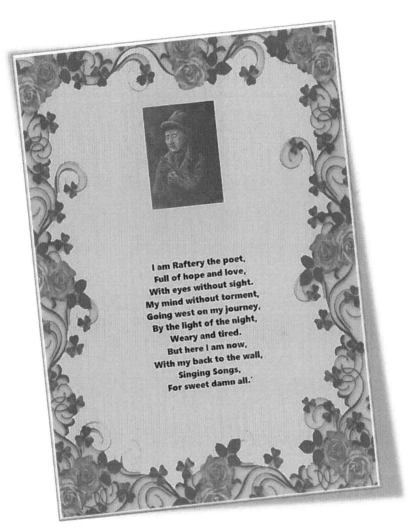

I am Raftery the poet,
Full of hope and love,
With eyes without sight.
My mind without torment,
Going west on my journey,
By the light of the night,
Weary and tired.
But here I am now,
With my back to the wall,
Singing Songs,
For sweet damn all.'

Figure 86 Anthony Raftery. Poet. circa 1779 to 1835

IN APPRECIATION TO JACKIE KELLY

If you do nothing, then nothing will happen.
The laptop is idle, do I have SOME fear?
That, to make a mistake, someone will hear,
Brand me a fool, be the subject of leer,
In front of the class, in the gaze of my peer(s).

When you do nothing expect nothing to happen
Our teacher was Jackie new life start was made,
Bade farewell to the pencil, the chalk, and the board,
Steady and slow, thru the Course we did wade,
With Jackie our mentor, you could not get bored.

Something to do, then something might happen.
With tea and the biscuits, we made our own craic,
The memory was rusty, but we are not! Going back,
And for many a time, it was repeat and remind,
Never mind says our Jackie, for she is always so kind.

Nothing will happen until you do something.
The first step is the hardest we're all in, the same boat,
'Remember Steve Jobs' So hang up your coat,
World window is open with the click of a mouse,
The Internet now, is all over the house,
To question, to query, and a library to 'fix it'
To Paint and to Snip is just part of your kit.

So! Do something and something will happen?
Goodbye to the old and hello to the new,
Excel and Access, to name but a few,
To upscale is now, the name of the game,
We aim for the top and the gold cup of fame,
Two clicks to the left, and one to the right,
Quiet Vatican bank and the might of the light.

To Jackie! I thank you from Paddy Walsh.

Made in the USA
Columbia, SC
22 February 2022

56285773R00080